P9-BYO-564

Volume 2

The Kids' World Almanac

OF RECORDS AND FACTS

Weekly Reader Books Presents

Volume 2

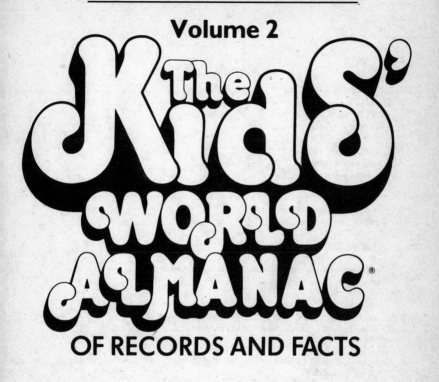

The Kids' WORLD ALMANAC

OF RECORDS AND FACTS

MARGO MCLOONE-BASTA AND ALICE SIEGEL

WORLD ALMANAC PUBLICATIONS
New York, New York

This book is a presentation of Weekly Reader Books.
Weekly Reader Books offers book clubs for children from
preschool through high school.

For further information write to:
Weekly Reader Books
4343 Equity Drive
Columbus, Ohio 43228

Book design: Blackbirch Graphics Inc.
Illustrations: Richard Rosenblum

Copyright © 1985 by Margo-Alice

All rights reserved. No part of this book may be reproduced in any
form or by any means without permission in writing by the
publisher.

Distributed in the United States by Ballantine Books, a division of
Random House, Inc. Distributed in Canada by Macmillan of Canada.

Newspaper Enterprise Association ISBN: 0-911818-65-0
Ballantine Books ISBN:

Printed in the United States of America

World Almanac Publications
Newspaper Enterprise Association
A division of United Media Enterprises
A Scripps Howard Company
200 Park Avenue
New York, New York 10166

Edited and abridged by Maria Burr for Weekly Reader
Book Club members.

Contents

ACKNOWLEDGMENTS

Our thanks to the many people in libraries, foundations, museums and organizations throughout the world who gave us their help. Special thanks to the following who provided particular help or inspiration. Our gratitude to Anna Basta, Douglas Basta, Vicky Beal, Daril Bentley, Nancy Bumpus, Miriam Chaikin, John F. Curtin, Carol DeMatteo, Debby Felder, Rob Fitz, June Foley, Mark Hoffman, Mike Madrid, Tom McGuire, Annie McLoone, Trish O'Connor, Leah Olivier, Laura Shucart, George Siegel, and Elyse Strongin.

Books and Magazines for Kids

A treasury of the favorite books of kids, classics for all time, magazines, and little known facts about books can be found here.

"There are more treasures in books than all the pirates' loot in Treasure Island. . . . and best of all, you can enjoy these riches every day of your life."
—WALT DISNEY

Book Bits

*In 300 B.C., Ptolemy I of Egypt founded a great library in Alexandria. The library did not contain books as we know them today—instead, it was filled with scrolls of papyrus. The library, which stood for over 400 years, was considered a cultural wonder of its time.

***The world's first printed book** was the Diamond Sutra. It was printed with wooden blocks and was published in China in 868 A.D.

***The most valuable book in the world** is the Gutenberg Bible which was first printed in 1455, in Mainz, Germany. This bible was the first book ever printed from moveable metal type. It is a huge book with 1,282 sheepskin pages which open to the width of a card table. In 1978 one of the 47 existing copies was sold for $2,400,000. Today, one copy is in the Library of Congress in the U.S., one is in the British Museum in England, and one is in the Biblioteque Nationale in France.

***The first children's book printed in English** was a book of rhymes entitled *A Book in Englyssh Metre of the Great Merchant Man Called Dives Pragmaticus*. It was printed by Alexander Lacy of England in 1563.

***The world's first children's magazine** was published in 1751 by John Newbery of England. The name of the magazine was *The Lilliputian*.

***The first children's library in America** was the Bingham Library for Youth in Salisbury, Connecticut. The library opened in 1803 with 150 books for kids aged 9 to 16 years old.

***The World Almanac** was first published in 1868. For a period of 10 years its annual publication was interrupted. In 1886 it was revived by publisher Joseph Pulitzer and has been printed every year thereafter.

***The first bookmobile** was a horse-drawn wagon filled with shelves to hold 250 books. These traveling libraries took books to readers in remote rural areas. The bookmobile was the idea and creation of a Maryland librarian in 1905.

***The world's largest collection of stored knowledge** is in the Library of Congress, a three-building complex in Washington, D.C. covering 82 acres. There are more than 18 million books, filling 535 miles of shelf space. There are more maps, globes,

charts, and atlases there than any other single place on earth.
Nearly every phonograph record ever made in the U.S. is kept
there. The largest collection of motion pictures in the world is
also in this library.

Children's Choices: The 25 Favorite Books
of American Kids

(SURVEY BY BOOKLIST MAGAZINE, 1982)

AUTHOR	TITLE
Blume, Judy	Superfudge
Blume, Judy	Tales of a Fourth Grade Nothing
Blume, Judy	Are You There, God? It's Me, Margaret
White, E.B.	Charlotte's Web
Blume, Judy	Blubber
Silverstein, Shel	Where the Sidewalk Ends
Farley, Walter	The Black Stallion
Dahl, Roald	Charlie and the Chocolate Factory
Rawls, Wilson	Where the Red Fern Grows
Blume, Judy	Deenie
Tolkien, J.R.R.	The Hobbit
Cleary, Beverly	Ramona the Pest
Blume, Judy	Forever
L'Engle, Madeleine	A Wrinkle in Time
Hinton, S.E.	The Outsiders
Wilder, Laura Ingalls	Little House on the Prairie
Blume, Judy	Tiger Eyes
Warner, Gertrude	The Boxcar Children
Cleary, Beverly	The Mouse and the Motorcycle
Rey, H.A.	Curious George
Lewis, C.S.	The Lion, the Witch and the Wardrobe
Rockwell, Thomas	How to Eat Fried Worms
Dahl, Roald	James and the Giant Peach
Silverstein, Shel	A Light in the Attic
Cleary, Beverly	Ramona Quimby, Age 8

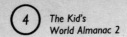

Fifty Contemporary Classics for Every Child

(COMPILED BY THE AMERICAN LIBRARY ASSOCIATION)

AUTHOR	TITLE
Alexander, Lloyd	The Book of Three
Babbitt, Natalie	Tuck Everlasting
Blume, Judy	Are You There, God? It's Me, Margaret
Bond, Michael	A Bear Called Paddington
Bond, Nancy	A String in the Harp
Boston, Lucy M.	The Children of Green Knowe
Byars, Betsy C.	The Midnight Fox
Cameron, Eleanor	The Court of the Stone Children
Cleary, Beverly	Ramona and Her Father
Cleaver, Vera and Cleaver, Bill	Where the Lilies Bloom
Collier, James L. and Collier, Christopher	My Brother Sam Is Dead
Cooper, Susan	The Dark Is Rising
Cresswell, Helen	Ordinary Jack: Being the First Part of the Bagthorpe Saga
de Jong, Meindert	House of Sixty Fathers
Donovan, John	Family
Fitgerald, John	The Great Brain
Fitzhugh, Louise	Harriet the Spy
Fleischman, Sid	Humbug Mountain
Fox, Paula	Slave Dancer
Greene, Bette	Summer of My German Soldier
Greene, Constance C.	Beat the Turtle Drum
Hamilton, Virginia	The Planet of Junior Brown
Holman, Felice	Slake's Limbo
Hunter, Mollie	A Stranger Came Ashore
Klein, Norma	Mom, the Wolf Man and Me
Konigsburg, E.L.	From the Mixed-Up Files of Mrs. Basil E. Frankweiler
Langton, Jane	The Fledgling
Le Guin, Ursula K.	A Wizard of Earthsea
L'Engle, Madeleine	A Wrinkle in Time
Lewis, C.S.	The Lion, the Witch and the Wardrobe
Lively, Penelope	The Ghost of Thomas Kempe
Lowry, Louis	Anastasia Krupnik

AUTHOR	TITLE
McKinley, Robin	Beauty: A Retelling of the Story of Beauty and the Beast
Mathis, Sharon B.	The Hundred Penny Box
Merrill, Jean	The Pushcart War
Norton, Mary	The Borrowers
O'Brien, Robert C.	Mrs. Frisby and the Rats of NIMH
O'Dell, Scott	Island of the Blue Dolphins
Paterson, Katherine	Bridge to Terabithia
Peck, Richard	The Ghost Belonged to Me
Pinkwater, Daniel	Lizard Music
Rockwell, Thomas	How to Eat Fried Worms
Rodgers, Mary	Freaky Friday
Selden, George	The Cricket in Times Square
Snyder, Zilpha K.	The Egypt Game
Speare, Elizabeth G.	The Witch of Blackbird Pond
Steig, William	Abel's Island
White, E.B.	Charlotte's Web
Wiseman, David	Jeremy Visick
Yep, Laurence	Dragonwings

Magazines for Kids

SUBJECT	TITLE	SUBSCRIPTION ADDRESS	FEATURES
Art	Art & Man (6 issues annually)	730 Broadway New York, NY 10003	Full color reproductions of art works; artist of the month; creative art projects.
Beauty; fashion	Seventeen (monthly)	850 Third Avenue New York, NY 10022	Short stories; articles; beauty and fashion tips.

SUBJECT	TITLE	SUBSCRIPTION ADDRESS	FEATURES
Computers	*Enter* (10 issues a year)	1 Lincoln Plaza New York, NY 10023	Only magazine of its kind for teens and pre-teens. Includes hardware and software, reviews, kids' columns and feature stories.
Consumer information	*Penny Power* (bi-monthly)	Consumers Union of U.S., Inc. P.O. Box 1906 Marion, OH 43302	How to be a wise consumer; how to manage your money.
Education/ entertainment	*Sesame Street* (10 issues a year)	Box 2896 Boulder, CO 80322	Sesame Street TV show characters; basic skills for pre-schoolers; "parents page."
Fashion	*Young Miss* (10 issues a year)	New Bridge Road Bergenfield, NJ 07621	Clothing and beauty tips; stories about friendship and romance.
Health	*Children's Digest* (9 issues a year)	1100 Waterway Blvd. P.O. Box 567 Indianapolis, IN 46206	Articles, puzzles and activities.
History	*Cobblestone* (monthly)	P.O. Box 959 Farmingdale, NY 11737	American history comes alive in themes which are related to historical dates of the month.
General interest	*Cricket* (monthly)	P.O. Box 2670 Boulder, CO 80322	A variety of stories from folk tales to science fiction.
General interest	*Lifeprints* (5 issues a year)	Blindskills Inc. P.O. Box 5181 Salem, OR 97304	This is a unique magazine for teens with limited eyesight or no sight at all. The magazine comes with large print, in braille, and in recorded casettes.
General interest	*Ebony Jr.* (monthly)	820 South Michigan Avenue Chicago, IL 60650	Stresses accomplishments of young blacks throughout the world.
General interest	*Highlights for Children* (11 issues a year)	P.O. Box 269 2300 West 5th Avenue Columbus, OH 43216	A broad range of topics from science and nature to space and math.

SUBJECT	TITLE	SUBSCRIPTION ADDRESS	FEATURES
General interest	*National Geographic World* (monthly)	National Geographic Society 17th and M Streets NW Washington, DC 20036	Factual stories about animals, sports, hobbies, and kids.
Music	*On Key* (6 issues a year)	JDL Publications P.O. Box 1213 Montclair, NJ 07042	Inspirational articles for young musicians.
Reading and writing	*Electric Company* (10 issues a year)	Box 2896 Boulder, CO 80322	Informative games, interviews and stories.
Recreation	*Boys' Life* (12 issues a year)	1325 Walnut Hill Lane Irving, TX 75062	Articles on sports, recreation, and scouting.
Science	*Odyssey* (monthly)	625 E. St. Paul Avenue P.O. Box 92788 Milwaukee, WI 53202	Articles on astronomy and outer space.
Science	*Owl* (10 issues a year)	59 Front Street East Toronto, Ontario Canada M5E1B3	Science stories from robots to the environment.
Science	*3-2-1 Contact* (10 issues a year)	Box 2896 Boulder, CO 80322	"Factoids" section; coming attractions in science; "Do It" section (puzzles, games); feature articles, including experiments.
Nature	*Ranger Rick's Nature Magazine* (monthly)	National Wildlife Foundation 1412 16th Street NW Washington, DC 20036	Emphasis on wildlife and the environment.
Writing	*Stone Soup* (5 issues a year)	Children's Art Fdtn. P.O. Box 83 Santa Cruz, CA 95063	Stories, book reviews, and artwork—all done by kids.

Bridges

The first people to live on earth were nomads who moved from place to place looking for food and shelter. They placed fallen trees across streams in order to pass from one side to the other. These trees were the first bridges. As civilization advanced so did the science of bridge building. New materials and techniques were used to build a variety of longer and stronger bridges. Modern man is able to span great bodies of water with spectacular bridges of steel and concrete.

Bridges inspire authors, poets, playwrights, artists, and photographers who praise them in words and pictures. Bridges are among the most complex, beautiful, and endearing structures built.

Major Types of Bridges

FIXED BRIDGES

Beam

This is the simplest type of bridge. It is constructed by laying beams of wood, steel, or concrete across an expanse. A simple example of this type of bridge is a fallen tree lying across a river with both ends resting on the river banks.

Cantilever

This bridge is made of three beams. Two beams are anchored to the two sides of the river bank. The third is placed between them to close the gap. Each of the anchored beams is called a cantilever.

Suspension

A suspension bridge is hung from two or more cables which pass over towers and are then anchored on both sides of the crossing. The first suspension bridges were tightropes strung across rivers.

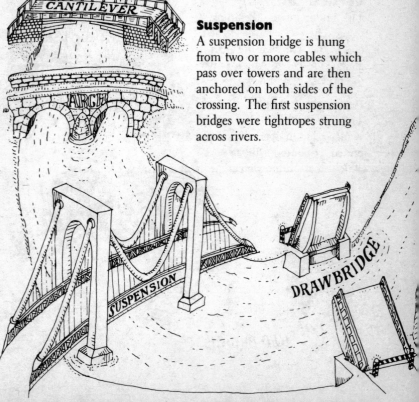

Arch

An arch bridge curves upward and the ends push outward against a support. It is considered to be an upside-down suspension bridge.

Covered

This is a wooden bridge with a roof built over it to protect it from rot caused by excessive moisture or dryness.

MOVABLE BRIDGES

Drawbridge

A drawbridge opens upward. The two ends are anchored and the center swings open.

Swing Span

A swing bridge opens outward. It is balanced by a pivot pier which is at its center.

Vertical Lift

This bridge moves like an elevator. There is a tower at each end of the span and the span is attached to cables which move the bridge up and down.

Pontoon Bridge

This is a floating bridge which swings aside to open. It is supported by pontoons (boats) which float on the water.

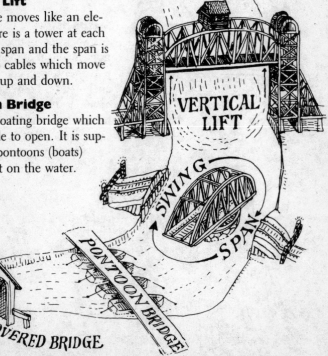

First in United States Bridges

1654   The first toll bridge in the U.S. was built over the New-bury River in Rowley, Massachusetts. The toll was charged for animals to cross. Pedestrians were allowed free passage.

1785   The first covered bridge was built over the Connecticut River in Bellows Fall, Vermont.

1796   The first suspension bridge was built over Jacob's Creek in Uniontown, Pennsylvania.

1804   The first pontoon bridge was built over Collins Pond in Lynn, Massachusetts.

1854   The first bridge to Canada was a suspension bridge built from Niagara Falls, New York.

1874   The first bridge across the Mississippi River was the Eads Bridge in St. Louis, Missouri.

1883   The first bridge with an elevated walkway was the Brooklyn Bridge which spans the East River in New York City. Pe-destrians cross the bridge on a promenade built above the roadway.

1883   The first bridge lighted by electricity was the Brooklyn Bridge.

1909   The first bridge with a double deck for traffic was the Queensborough Bridge across the East River in New York City.

1976   The first bridge named after a woman was the Betsy Ross Bridge across the Delaware River in Philadelphia, Pennsyl-vania. (Legend has it that Betsy Ross, a seamstress during the American Revolution, made the first national flag for the United States government.)

Bridge Bests

Costliest   The **Verrazano-Narrows Bridge** over New York Bay is the most expensive bridge ever built. It was completed in 1964 at a cost of $304,000,000.

Most Famous	**Old London Bridge**, which spanned the Thames River in England, is considered the most famous bridge in the English-speaking world.
Heaviest Load Carrying	**Hell Gate Bridge** over the East River in New York City can withstand the heaviest load of traffic. Built in 1917 for railroad traffic, it can hold up 24,000 pounds per foot, or a 10,000-ton spread.
Highest	**The Royal Gorge Bridge** was built 1,053 feet above the Arkansas River in central Colorado. It is the highest bridge above water in the world.
Longest	**The Lake Ponchartrain No. 2** in New Orleans, Louisiana, is the world's longest bridge. It is 23.87 miles long. Eight miles of the bridge are out of sight of land. The bridge, which spans Lake Ponchartrain, was completed in 1969.
Tallest	**The Golden Gate Bridge** over San Francisco Bay in San Francisco, California, is the tallest bridge in the world. The towers of this suspension bridge extend 745 feet up above the water.

THE WORLD'S LONGEST BRIDGES

TYPE	NAME	LOCATION	LENGTH	DATE COMPLETED
Arch	New River Gorge	U.S.A., Fayetteville, West Virginia	1,700 ft.	1977
Bascule	Pearl River	U.S.A., Sidell, Louisiana	482 ft.	1969
Beam	Lake Ponchartrain Number 2	U.S.A., over Lake Ponchartrain, New Orleans, Louisiana	23.87 mi.	1969
Cantilever	Quebec Railway Bridge	Canada, over the St. Lawrence River, Quebec City	1,800 ft.	1917
Covered	Hartland Bridge	Canada, New Brunswick Province	1,282 ft.	1899

TYPE	NAME	LOCATION	LENGTH	DATE COMPLETED
Pontoon	Evergreen Point Bridge	U.S.A., over Lake Washington, Seattle, Washington	7,518 ft.	1961
Suspension	Humber Bridge	U.K., over the Humbe Estuary in Hull, England	4,626 ft.	1977
Swing Span	El Ferdan Bridge	Egypt, over the Suez Canal	552 ft.	1965
Vertical Lift	Arthur Kill Bridge	U.S.A., over the Arthur Channel in Elizabeth, New Jersey	558 ft.	1959

Fascinating Facts About Bridges

FIVE BRIDGES MADE FAMOUS IN LITERATURE

Boston Bridge in Boston, Massachusetts, is the subject of "Bridge Over the Charles," a poem by Henry Wadsworth Longfellow.
Brooklyn Bridge in New York City is the setting of "A View from The Bridge," a play by Arthur Miller.
Drina Bridge in Visegard, Yugoslavia, is the subject of *The Bridge on the Drina*, a Nobel prize-winning novel by Ivo Andue.
Old London Bridge in London, England is the subject of "London Bridge Is Falling Down," a nursery rhyme.
Quebec Bridge in Quebec, Canada, is the subject of *Alexander's Bridge*, a novel by Willa Cather.

FIVE BRIDGES MADE FAMOUS IN MOVIES

The Bridge of San Luis Rey is a 1945 movie based on a novel of the same name by Thornton Wilder. It is about the collapse of a primitive suspension bridge built by the Inca indians in the Andes mountains of Peru.

The Bridges at Tokyo-Ri is a 1954 war movie about the destruction of four North Korean military bridges.

The Bridge on the River Kwai is a 1957 movie about a railroad bridge built in Siam (now Thailand), by a British colonel captured by the Japanese in World War II.

The Bridge is a 1959 movie about an unnamed bridge defended during World War II by a group of German school boys.

The Bridge at Remagen is a 1969 movie about the bridge across the Rhine River that the allied forces crossed into Germany. The crossing became a turning point in World War II.

FIVE BRIDGES WITH UNUSUAL NAMES

Bridge of Boils—Lima, Peru

An epidemic of bubonic plague broke out among the workmen while they were building this bridge. The disease is characterized by boils (made by the swelling of the lymph nodes). The bridge was named Puente de las Verrugus—the Bridge of Boils.

Bridge of Sighs—Venice, Italy

This bridge was named for the sighs of unhappy prisoners who used it to cross from their prison to the palace where they were sentenced for their crimes.

Hell Gate Bridge—New York City, U.S.A.

The waters beneath this bridge are so turbulent and treacherous they have been likened to the gates of Hell. Thus, the name Hell Gate Bridge.

Honeymoon Bridge—Niagara Falls, New York, U.S.A.

This bridge was located in the one-time "honeymoon capital of America." Because of the number of married couples who honeymooned in Niagara Falls, the bridge was named the Honeymoon Bridge. It was destroyed in 1938 by an ice jam and replaced by the Rainbow Bridge.

Outerbridge—Staten Island, New York, U.S.A.

It is commonly believed that this bridge was named Outerbridge because of its remoteness from the center of New York City. It was actually named after Eugenius Outerbridge, the first chairman of New York's Port Authority.

FIVE FAMOUS BRIDGE DISASTERS

Tay Bridge Over The Firth Of Tay, Scotland

On December 28, 1979, the bridge collapsed due to a combination of gale winds and faulty construction. A passenger train with 75 people aboard fell into the inlet. There were no survivors.

Quebec Bridge Over The St. Laurence River, Quebec City, Canada

On August 29, 1907, while the bridge was under construction, part of it collapsed and 82 workers died.

Tacoma Narrows Bridge Over Puget Sound, Tacoma, Washington

On November 7, 1940, only four months after this bridge was completed, it collapsed from the force of gale winds. There were no lives lost.

Sunshine Skyway Bridge Over Tampa Bay, St. Petersburg, Florida

On May 9, 1980, an ocean freighter smashed into an abutment of the bridge. Three cars, one truck and one bus plummetted into the water. Thirty-five people were killed.

Connecticut Turnpike Bridge Over The Mianus River, Greenwich, Connecticut

On June 28, 1983, the bridge collapsed due to disrepair, and three motorists were killed. The collapse of this roadway, an important gateway to New England from New York, resulted in major traffic disruption for months.

FIVE CITIES KNOWN FOR THEIR BRIDGES		FIVE STATES IN THE U.S. WITH THE MOST COVERED BRIDGES	
New York, NY., U.S.A.	1,420 bridges	Pennsylvania	347 bridges
Sydney, Australia	1,305 bridges	Ohio	234 bridges
Venice, Italy	450 bridges	Indiana	152 bridges
Amsterdam, Holland	300 bridges	Vermont	121 bridges
Osaka, Japan	250 bridges	Oregon	106 bridges

FIVE BRIDGES MADE FAMOUS IN PAINTINGS

Pont-Neuf Bridge in Paris, painted by Renoir.
Pont St. Michel Bridge in Paris, painted by Matisse.
A Vermont Covered Bridge, painted by Grandma Moses.
Waterloo Bridge in London, painted by Monet
Westminster Bridge in London, painted by Whistler.

FIVE NOTABLE AMERICAN BRIDGE BUILDERS

BUILDER	BRIDGE	DATE COMPLETED
O.H. Ammann	Outerbridge, Staten Island, N.Y.	1928
	Bayonne Bridge, Bayonne, N.J.	1931
	George Washington Bridge, New York, N.Y.	1931
	Golden Gate Bridge, San Francisco, Ca.	1937
	Verrazano-Narrows Bridge, N.Y.	1969
James Buchanan Eads	St. Louis or Eads Bridge, St. Louis, Mo.	1874
Roebling John (Father) and Washington (Son)	Allegheny River Bridge, Pittsburgh, Pa.	1845
	Niagara River Railroad Bridge, Niagara Falls, N.Y.	1865
	Ohio River Bridge, Cincinnati, Oh.	1866
	Brooklyn Bridge, N.Y., N.Y.	1883
David Steinman	Florianopolis Bridge, Brazil	1926
	Carquinez Strait Bridge, Ca.	1927
	Sydney Harbor Bridge, Australia	1932
	Triboro Bridge, N.Y., N.Y.	1936
	Mackinac Straits Bridge, Mi.	1957

Contests for Kids

Can you catch a greasy pig? How many hot dogs can you eat in one sitting? Can you spell *aardvark?* If the answer to any of these questions is yes, there is a contest for you.

"The Apple Seed Popping Contest"

Contestants are given fresh apples to squeeze in their fists. The one who pops the apple seeds the farthest wins. There is also an Apple Core Throwing Contest in which contestants line up and attempt to throw the apple core the farthest.

PRIZE: Trophies
AGE: 16 and under
LOCATION: Lincoln, Nebraska
DATE: First weekend in
   October, annually.

"Seventeen Magazine's Annual Art Contest"

Entrants submit one or two samples of artwork by mail. The samples may be no larger than 20 by 26 inches. Each sample must have the entrant's name, address, telephone number, and birth date (month and year) written on the back. A panel of judges selects the winners on the basis of skill, originality, and suitability for publication in the magazine.

PRIZES: Cash to top three
   winners
AGE: 13 to 20 years old
DATE: Annually
CONTACT:
   Art Contest
   Seventeen Magazine
   850 Third Avenue
   New York, New York
   10022

"The Banana Eating Contest"

The contestant who can consume the most bananas in an allotted time, wins the contest.

PRIZES: Ribbons and
   bananas
LOCATION: Fulton, Kentucky
DATE: August, annually
CONTACT:
   International Banana
   Festival
   P.O. 428
   Fulton, Kentucky 42041

"America's Bake-Off Contest"

Contestants must submit, in writing, an original recipe using specified Pillsbury products. One hundred and ten finalists are chosen to attend (expenses paid). Each finalist prepares his or her own recipe. The winning recipes are selected for their taste and appearance.

PRIZES: Cash (up to $40,000
   for the Grand Prize
   winner)
AGE: 10 years and over

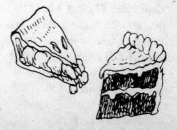

LOCATION: A major U.S. city is selected for each contest.

DATES: About every two years

CONTACT:
Pillsbury Company
Consumer Affairs
Box 550
Minneapolis, Minnesota
55440

"The Bubble Gum Blowing Contest"

Each contestant is provided with one stick of bubble gum to be used in the 3 events of this contest: First to Blow a Bubble, Biggest Bubble Blown, Longest Lasting Bubble.

PRIZES: Gum and paperback books

AGE: 5 to 12 years

LOCATION: Main Library, Albany, Oregon

DATE: July, annually

CONTACT:
Children's Librarian
Albany Public Library
1390 Waverly Drive, S.E.
Albany, Oregon 97312

"Chicken Flying Meet"

The contestants enter their own chicken in one of four weight classes. Each chicken is placed on a roost or launching pad and must take flight within 30 seconds of the starting signal. Chickens may be gently nudged to fly. The flight of the chicken is measured from the base of the roost to the point where the chicken first touches down. The winning chickens fly the longest distance within the flight area.

PRIZES: Cash to the top three contestants in each weight class

AGE: No age limit for chickens or owners

LOCATION: Bob Evans Farm, Rio Grande, Ohio

DATE: Third Saturday in May, annually

CONTACT:
International Chicken
Flying Meet Secretary
3776 South High Street
Columbus, Ohio 43207

"The Conch Shell Blowing Contest"

Contestants bring their own conch shell to compete in this event. There are five age divisions and the winner in each division is selected by a panel of judges for the tone and quality of their blowing. Each contestant performs on stage before an audience.

PRIZES: Trophies

AGE: 4 divisions within the 3 to 17 year old range, and 18 years and over

LOCATION: Key West, Florida

DATE: Last two weeks of March, annually
CONTACT:
"Old Island Days"
Key West, Florida 33040

"World Championship Crab Races"

Contestants may bring their own crab or rent one at the contest site. The crabs, prodded by whistlers, blowing or screams, race down a 5-foot track. Contestants are not allowed to touch the crabs during the race. The first crabs to cross the finish line are the winners.

PRIZES: Trophies and cash
AGE: Juniors—under 12 years
Adults—over 12 years
LOCATION: Crescent City, California
DATE: Sunday of Washington's Birthday weekend, annually

"The Advanced Dungeons and Dragons Fantasy and Role-Playing Game"

Contestants compete for the title of champion "Dungeon Master." They must create an original pencil and paper design of a dungeon filled with monsters, treasures, tricks, and traps. Each contestant plays a game of the imagination with the judges. The game is played inside the dungeon designed by the contestant. The judges select the winner on the basis of dungeon design and role-playing.

PRIZES: Trophies
AGE: No Limit
DATE: Annually
CONTACT:
T.S.R. Hobbies, Inc.
P.O. Box 726
Lake Geneva, Wisconsin 53147

"Junior World Duck-Calling Contest"

Contestants attempt to reproduce vocally four kinds of duck calls: comeback call, feed call, hail call, and mating call. The winners are selected by a panel of judges.

PRIZES: Cash
AGE: 14 and under
LOCATION: Stuttgart, Arkansas
DATE: November 25, annually
ENTRY FEE: $12.00

"The White House Easter Egg Roll"

Thousands of contestants wait in line to participate in this event. Eight kids compete at one time, each using a spoon to push a colored egg down an 8-foot lane. One in every 8 is a winner and all entrants receive prizes.

PRIZES: Each contestant is given a remembrance for participating.

AGE: 8 years old and under, accompanied by an adult

LOCATION: South lawn of White House, Washington, D.C.

DATE: Monday after Easter Sunday, annually

"Fence Painting, National Tom Sawyer Day"

Contestants for the event are selected by local contests held in their home states. Judges for the national championship score each contestant in three categories: costume (authentic Tom Sawyer garb), speed (how fast contestant white washes a 4' × 5' fence and runs to finish line), and painting quality (uniformity and coverage of whitewash).

PRIZES: Cash and traveling Trophy displayed in the state capitol building of winner

AGE: 10 through 13

LOCATION: Hannibal, Missouri

DATE: Fourth of July, annually

CONTACT:
Hannibal Jaycees
P.O. Box 484
Hannibal, Missouri 63401

"International Frog Racing & Jumping Contest"

Contestants may enter their own frog or rent a frog at the contest site. The frogs allowed in the competition are bullfrogs, toadfrogs and springfrogs, measuring 4 inches from nose to tail. The first to cross the finish line in the frog race, wins. The frogs may be coaxed with dull-edged instruments. In the Jumping Contest the frog that jumps the furthest distance in 3 jumps, wins.

PRIZES: Trophies
AGE: No limit
LOCATION: Payne, Louisiana
DATE: Saturday of third
weekend in September,
annually

"The Greasy Pig Scramble"

Each contestant tries to catch a
pig greased with peanut oil,
hold on to it, and drag it across
the finish line. The first one to
succeed wins the contest.

PRIZE: The pig
AGE: 14 and under
LOCATION: Dothan, Alabama
DATE: Mid-October
CONTACT:
Peanut Festival
Dothan, Alabama 36302

"The Hot Dog Eating Contest"

Contestants are provided with
hot dogs and the winner is the
one who can eat the most hot
dogs within a certain time
limit.

PRIZE: Ribbons
AGE: No age limit
LOCATION:
Nathan's at Coney Island
1310 Surf Avenue
Brooklyn, New York 11224
DATE: Fourth of July,
annually

"International Juggler Association's Junior Championship"

The juggling contest is a staged
event held in a theatre. An
audience and a panel of 7
judges watch a 3-minute free
style performance by each contestant. The winner is selected
for juggling ability, stage presentation, and costume.

PRIZE: Trophy
AGE: 16 and under
LOCATION: Annual I.J.A.
convention site
DATE: Third week of July,
annually
CONTACT:
I.J.A.
P.O. Box 383
New York, New York 10040

"The World Championship Log Rolling Contest"

Contestants in this event compete two at a time, in a series
of eliminations. The contestants try to maintain their bal-
ance on a floating log. The
winners are the ones who stay
on the log after their opponents
topple into the water. The contestant who "out-rolls" all the
competitors is the champion.

PRIZES: Trophies
AGE:
Juniors: 9 and under
Intermediates: 10–13

Seniors: 14–18
LOCATION: Hayward, Wisconsin
DATE: Last weekend in July,
annually
CONTACT:
Telemark Lodge
Hayward, Wisconsin 54843

"The National Marbles Tournament"

Boys and girls compete separately in this tournament. Each contestant must qualify for the competition by first winning local tournaments. "Ringers" is the contest game. The champion in each division must win a series of round robin play.

PRIZES: Trophies
AGE: 14 and under
LOCATION: Wildwood, New
Jersey
DATE: Last week of June,
annually
CONTACT:
Chamber of Commerce
Wildwood, New Jersey
08260

"Now You're Cooking Contest"

Contestants submit a planned menu, using specific food products. There are four categories of competition: Dinner for Two, Family Dinner, American Regional, and Party for Friends. Contestants mail their menus (each entrant must have a school sponsor whose signature accompanies the entry). Six finalists are chosen in each category. They travel, expenses paid, to the "cook-off," which is held at the Culinary Institute of America. The winners are selected for the taste, appearance, originality, nutrition, and creativity of their menus.

PRIZES: Cash and school
tuition
AGE: 13 through 19
LOCATION: Hyde Park, New
York
DATE: Fall, annually
CONTACT:
Seventeen Magazine
Education Division
850 Third Avenue
New York, New York 10022

"The Milk Drinking Contest"

The contestant who can drink a container of milk in the quickest time wins the contest. The entrants compete within specified age divisions.

PRIZES: Ribbons
AGE: 3 to 18 (3 divisions)
LOCATION: Los Angeles
County Fair
Los Angeles, California
DATE: End of September,
annually
CONTACT:
Milk Drinking Contest

(L.A. Fair)
P.O. Box 388
Industry City, California
   91747

"The Peanut Recipe Contest"

Contestants submit an original recipe using peanuts. Fifteen finalists are selected to bring in their prepared recipe. A panel of judges selects a winner on the basis of taste and appearance.

PRIZES: Cash
AGE: 16 and under
LOCATION: Dothan, Alabama
DATE: Mid-October
CONTACT:
   National Peanut Festival
      Association
   Dothan, Alabama 36302

"The Pet Rock Race and Costume Contest"

Contestants race their own rocks down a 16-foot incline. The owner of the rock that rolls the furthest, without rolling off course, wins the race. In the Best-Dressed Rock Contest, a panel of judges selects the rock with the most creative garb.

PRIZES: Cash, trophies, ribbons
AGE: 3 divisions: under 10, 10–13, 14–18
LOCATION:
   Logan County Fair
   Logan, Colorado
DATE: Beginning of August, annually

"The National Rotten Sneaker Championship"

Contestants wear their naturally-worn sneakers and parade in front of a panel of judges. Ten finalists are selected. They must jump up and down in front of judges to prove wearability of sneakers. The judges select the most rotten, yet wearable, pair of sneakers.

PRIZES: New sneakers and foot powder
AGE: Under 18
LOCATION: Montpelier, Vermont
DATE: First day of Spring
CONTACT:
   Recreation Department
   Montpelier, Vermont
      05602

"The Sun Herald Sand Sculpture Contest for Scouts"

Teams of Boy Scouts and Girl Scouts participate in this event. The sculptures must relate to the theme of that year's contest. Contestants are provided with a limited area of space and are given five hours to create their sculptures. A panel of judges determines winners based on creativity and execution.

PRIZES: Trophies and cash to winning troop
AGE: Cub Scouts, Brownies, Boy Scouts, Girl Scouts
LOCATION: Biloxi, Mississippi
DATE: Third week in September, annually
CONTACT:
    Gulf Publishing, Inc.
    Director of Marketing
    Biloxi, Mississippi 39530

"The National Sewing Month Contest"

Entrants compete in one of two contest categories: apparel and crafts. A 5" × 7" photo of the entry must be mailed with an entry form (available at sewing stores throughout the country) to the contest site. Twenty-five finalists are chosen in each category and in each age division. Their finished products are mailed to the contest site where a panel of judges selects win-ners for creativity and sewing ability.

PRIZES: Cash
AGE: 14 and under, 15 to 21, and 3 older divisions
DATE: September through November, annually
CONTACT:
    American Home Sewing Association
    Suite 1007
    1270 Broadway
    New York, New York 10001

"The World Championship Snow Shovel Riding Contest"

Each contestant must ride a coal shovel down a 153-foot snow-covered hill. The one with the fastest time wins. Boys and girls compete separately.

PRIZES: Trophies
AGE: 13 and under
LOCATION: Ambridge, Pennsylvania
DATE: Third week in January
CONTACT:
    Beaver County Tourist Prom. Agency
    14th and Church Street
    Ambridge, Pennsylvania 15003

"All American Soap Box Derby"

Contestants race their home-made soap box derby cars down

a 953-foot course. The wooden or fiberglass cars must be built to specifications listed in the official rule book. All contestants must first win local races in order to compete.

PRIZES: Scholarships, trophies, jackets, helmets and T-shirts; a week at Derby Downs Camp
AGE: 2 divisions, Junior 10–12, Senior 12–15
LOCATION: Derby Downs, Akron, Ohio
DATE: Second Saturday of August, annually
CONTACT:
All American Soap Box Derby
789 Derby Downs Drive
Akron, Ohio 44309

"The National Spelling Bee"

Contestants are asked to spell, out loud, a series of words. The entrant who "out-spells" the others wins. Every contestant is sponsored by a daily or weekly newspaper and he or she must win local and regional spelling bees to compete in the national contest.

PRIZES: Trophies
AGE: Under 16
LOCATION: Washington, D.C.
DATE: Late May, early June, annually
CONTACT:
National Spelling Bee
1100 Central Trust Tower
Cincinnati, Ohio 45202

"Seventeen Magazine's Fiction Contest"

Entrants submit original stories between 1,000 and 3,000 words in length by mail. The stories must be typed (double spaced) with the name and address of the entrant on each page. There is no limit to the number of stories each contestant may submit. The editors of the magazine select the winners on the basis of literary worth, originality, naturalness of dialogue, characterization, and suitability for publication in the magazine.

PRIZES: Cash to the top three winners; six honorable mentions
AGE: 13 through 19
DATE: Summer, annually
CONTACT:
Fiction Contest
Seventeen Magazine
850 Third Avenue
New York, New York 10022

"The Ugly Dog Contest"

Contestants bring their ugly dogs to this event where a panel of judges select the ugliest dogs in two categories: Mutt and Pedigree. The two winners may return the following year to participate in the "Ring of Champions" where mutt and pedigree dogs compete together for the title of "The Ugliest Dog."

PRIZES: Trophies
LOCATION: Petaluma, California
DATE: Springtime, annually
CONTACT:
Chamber of Commerce
Petaluma, California 94952

"Atari's Video Game Contest"

Each year a video game by Atari is selected for tournament competition. Contestants participate in a series of eliminations. Winners are determined by the highest scores. The top six contestants in each category advance to the finals.

PRIZES: Cash
AGE: Juniors: 18 and under
Seniors: 18 and over
DATE: No set date
LOCATION: Major cities throughout the world are selected for each year's tournament
CONTACT:
Atari Inc.
1265 Borregas Avenue
P.O. Box 427
Sunnyvale, California 94086

Fifty Questions
Kids Ask Most

(According to the American Library Association)

1. **How much does the earth weigh?**
   ANSWER: Six sextillion, 588 quintillion short tons (a short ton equals 2,000 pounds).
   SOURCE: *Van Nostrand's Scientific Encyclopedia.*

2. **What is the highest city in the world?**
   ANSWER: Lhasa, Tibet, which is 12,002 feet above sea level.
   SOURCE: Kurian, George Thomas; *The Book of World Rankings.*

3. **Who was the real St. Nicholas?**
   ANSWER: He is thought to be the Bishop of Myra, who lived in Asia Minor during the 4th century.
   SOURCE: Myers, Robert J., *Celebrations: The Complete Book of American Holidays.*

4. **How many copies must be sold of a record for it to be awarded a gold record? a platinum record?**
   ANSWER: In the U.S., Gold Records are awarded to single records that sell one million copies; Platinum Records are awarded to those selling two million copies.
   SOURCE: *The World Almanac and Book of Facts 1984*

5. **Which first lady was cross-eyed?**
   ANSWER: Julia Dent Grant, the wife of Ulysses S. Grant.
   SOURCE: Bassett, Margaret; *Profiles and Portraits of American Presidents and Their Wives.*

6. **What does "Triskaidekaphobia" mean?**
   ANSWER: Fear of the number 13.
   SOURCE: *Webster's Third New International Dictionary.*

7. **What is the largest animal that is living today?**
   ANSWER: The blue whale, which can weigh up to 209 tons.
   SOURCE: *Guinness Book of World Records;* 1984 edition.

8. **What is the difference between "adsorption" and "absorption"?**
   ANSWER: Adsorption is the assimiliation of gas, vapor, or dissolved matter by the surface of a solid or liquid. Absorption is the act or process of absorbing or the condition of being absorbed, e.g., soaking up.

9. **What makes popcorn "pop"?**
   ANSWER: Popcorn is different from other kinds of corn because its kernels have a hard, tough waterproof covering. When popcorn kernels are heated, this covering keeps the natural moisture inside the kernels from escaping. If the kernels are heated enough, this moisture turns to steam and actually explodes the kernels.
   SOURCE: *The New Book of Knowledge;* 1982, volume "C."

10. **What does the word "pixilated" mean?**
    ANSWER: Pixilated means somewhat unbalanced mentally; also bemused or whimsical.
    SOURCE: *Webster's Ninth New Collegiate Dictionary;* 1983.

11. **What is the relationship between George Washington and Robert E. Lee?**

    ANSWER: Robert E. Lee was married to Martha Washington's great-granddaughter.

    SOURCE: *World Book Encyclopedia*; 1984, Vol. 12.

12. **What song is known as the Black National Anthem?**

    ANSWER: "Lift Every Voice and Sing" by James Weldon Johnson.

    SOURCE: *The Negro Almanac: A Reference Work on the Afro-American*, edited by Harry A. Ploski and James Williams, 4th edition, 1983.

13. **Who invented the pencil?**

    ANSWER: The ancient Greeks and Romans first used writing tools made of lead shortly before the birth of Christ. The first graphite pencils were made by the English in the mid-1500s. About 1650, the Germans enclosed the piece of graphite in a wooden case.

    SOURCE: *World Book Encyclopedia*; 1984, Vol. 15.

14. **Who were the nine muses?**

    ANSWER: In Greek mythology, the nine daughters of Zeus, king of the gods, and Mnemosyne, goddess of memory, were the nine goddesses of the arts and sciences. Calliope was the muse of epic poetry; Erato, of love poetry; Euterpe, of lyric poetry; Melpomene, of tragedy; Thalia, of comedy; Clio, of history; Urania, of astronomy; Polyhymnia, of sacred song; and Terpischore, of dance.

    SOURCE: *World Book Encyclopedia*; 1984, Vol. 13.

STATUE OF ZEUS

15. **When was the first Mother's Day?**
    ANSWER: The first Mother's Day was celebrated in Philadelphia on May 10, 1908. In 1914, President Woodrow Wilson issued a proclamation asking all citizens to give a public expression of reverence to mothers. In the U.S. it is celebrated on the second Sunday in May.
    SOURCE: Gregory, Ruth; *Anniversaries and Holidays*.

16. **Who was the first woman doctor?**
    ANSWER: Elizabeth Blackwell.
    SOURCE: Crook, Bette; *Famous Firsts in Medicine*.

17. **What do you feed a crayfish?**
    ANSWER: Snails, small fish, tadpoles, and young insects.
    SOURCE: *World Book Encyclopedia*; 1984, Vol. 4.

18. **What is the history of the yo-yo?**
    ANSWER: Yo-yos began as weapons in the hands of early inhabitants of the primeval jungles of the Philippines. The word comes from the Philippine word meaning "to return." Since then, the yo-yo has appeared in many cultures and the toy has been called many other names.
    SOURCE: Olney, Ross; *The Amazing Yo-Yo*.

19. **Who was the first honorary United States citizen?**
    ANSWER: British prime minister, Winston Churchill in 1963.
    SOURCE: *World Book Encyclopedia*; 1984, Vol. 3.

20. **Who is the illustrator behind Marvel Comics?**
    ANSWER: Stan Lee.
    SOURCE: *The World Encyclopedia of Comics*.

21. **What are the statistics for the suicide rates of teenagers?**
    ANSWER: The rates per 100,000 people between the ages of 15 and 24 are 5.2% in 1960, 8.8% in 1970, 12.5% in 1980, and 13.0% in 1981.
    SOURCE: *U.S. News and World Report*, June 20, 1983.

22. **What does the word "ginnel" mean?**
    ANSWER: A narrow passage or entry between buildings; an alley.
    SOURCE: Wright, Joseph; *English Dialect Dictionary, Vol. 2*.

23. **Where is the U.S. Space Camp for Children?**
    ANSWER: Near the Alabama Space and Rocket Center, Huntsville, Alabama.
    SOURCE: *National Geographic World*, May 1983.

24. **In what year did the modern Olympics begin?**
    ANSWER: 1896.
    SOURCE: Giller, Norman; *The 1984 Olympics Handbook*.

25. **What is the tallest building in the world?**
    ANSWER: The Sears Tower in Chicago Illinois (110 stories, 1,454 feet).
    SOURCE: *Childcraft—The How and Why Library*.

26. **What was Dr. Seuss' first published children's book?**
    ANSWER: *And to Think That I Saw It on Mulberry Street* (Vanguard, 1937).
    SOURCE: Commire, Anne; *Something About the Author*.

27. **What was the first state to ratify the Constitution?**
    ANSWER: Delaware, on December 7, 1787.
    SOURCE: *The Encyclopedia of American Facts and Dates*; edited by Gordire Carruth and Associates.

28. **Which state was the first to abolish slavery?**
    ANSWER: Vermont, on July 1, 1777.
    SOURCE: *The Encyclopedia of American Facts and Dates*; edited by Gordire Carruth and Associates.

29. **What were the Marx Brothers' real names?**
    ANSWER: Chico—Leonard; Harpo—Adolph; Groucho—Julius;
    Zeppo—Herbert; Gummo—Milton.
    SOURCE: *The Oxford Companion to Film*; edited by Liz-Anne Bawden.

30. **What is Cinco de Mayo?**
    ANSWER: A Mexican holiday recognizing the anniversary of the Battle of Puebla, May 5, 1862, in which Mexican troops, outnumbered three to one, defeated the invading French troops of Napoleon III.

SOURCE: Chase, William D. and Helen; *Chase's Annual Events*.

31. **Who discovered Cleveland?**
ANSWER: Moses Cleaveland, an agent of the Connecticut Land Company, laid out the town in 1796.
SOURCE: *Dictionary of American History*.

32. **Where is Swahili spoken?**
ANSWER: In the African countries of Kenya, Tanzania, Zaire, Uganda, Somalia, and Mozambique.
SOURCE: *World Book Encyclopedia*; 1973, Vol. 18.

33. **Who said "Don't Give Up the Ship"?**
ANSWER: Captain James Lawrence on board the U.S. frigate, *Chesapeake*, on June 1, 1813.
SOURCE: *Bartlett's Familiar Quotations*.

34. **What is the smallest mainland nation in the Western Hemisphere?**
ANSWER: El Salvador, which covers only 8,123 square miles.
SOURCE: Wallechinsky, David and Irving Wallace; *The People's Almanac 2*.

35. **When did The Today Show go on the air?**
ANSWER: January 16, 1952.
SOURCE: Wallechinsky, David and Irving Wallace; *The People's Almanac 2*.

36. **What was the Black Sox Scandal?**
ANSWER: In 1919 eight members of the Chicago White Sox baseball team accepted bribes to "fix" the World Series between the Cincinnati Reds and the White Sox. When the case went to trial in 1921, the eight were acquitted. However, Baseball Commissioner Kenesaw Mountain Landis barred the eight players from professional baseball for life.
SOURCE: Wallechinsky, David and Irving Wallace; *The People's Almanac 2*.

37. **What are the categories for the Nobel Prize?**
ANSWER: Awards have been given for Literature, Physics, Chemistry, Physiology and Medicine, and Peace since 1901. In 1969 the sixth award, for Economics was first given.
SOURCE: *The Concise Columbia Encyclopedia*.

38. **When did people in America start paying income taxes?**
    ANSWER: During the Civil War the U.S. imposed a tempo-
    rary income tax; the system became permanent with the
    adoption of the Sixteenth Amendment to the Constitution
    in 1913.
    SOURCE: *The Concise Columbia Encyclopedia*.

39. **What is a swastika?**
    ANSWER: The swastika is an ancient symbol which was used
    as an ornament or a religious sign. It is in the form of a
    cross with the ends of the arms bent at right angles in a
    given direction, usually clockwise. Swastikas were widely-
    used symbols among the Indians of North and South
    America. It was adopted as the symbol of the National
    Socialist Party (NAZIS) in Germany in 1920 and came to
    stand for all evil associated with the Nazis during World
    War II.
    SOURCE: *World Book Encyclopedia*; 1984, Vol. 18.

40. **What is the coldest temperature ever recorded in the conti-
    nental United States? the hottest?**
    ANSWER: The coldest recorded temperature was −70° Fahr-
    enheit (−57° Celsius) recorded on January 13, 1971 at
    Prospect Creek Camp, Alaska. The hottest recorded tem-
    perature was 124°F. (57° Celsius) recorded on July 10,
    1913 in Death Valley, California.
    SOURCE: *The American Weather Book*.

41. **Is there really a Swan Lake?**
    ANSWER: Even though the lake in Tchaikovsky's ballet is fic-
    tional, there are at least six small lakes named Swan Lake
    located in British Columbia, Manitoba, Montana, South
    Dakota, Utah, and New York.

42. **What is Robert C. O'Brien's (author of *Mrs. Frisby and the
    Rats of NIMH*) real name?**
    ANSWER: Robert Leslie Conly.
    SOURCE: *Twentieth Century Children's Writers*; edited by
    D. L. Kirkpatrick.

43. **When is Bill Peet's birthday and is he still alive?**
    ANSWER: January 29, and yes.
    SOURCE: *Twentieth Century Children's Writers*; edited by
    D. L. Kirkpatrick.

44. **What causes hiccups?**
   ANSWER: A sudden involuntary intake of air caused by a
      spasm of the diaphragm.
   SOURCE: *World Book Encyclopedia*; 1984, Vol. 9.

45. **Who was the first non-native child born in America?**
   ANSWER: The first child born of English parents in New Eng-
      land was Peregrine White, born on board the Mayflower as
      she lay at anchor at Cape Cod Bay on November 20, 1620.
   SOURCE: *Famous First Facts.*

46. **What was the earliest animated 3-D cartoon?**
   ANSWER: The first animated three-dimensional cartoon in
      Technicolor was Walt Disney's *Melody.* Its world premiere
      took place on May 28, 1953.
   SOURCE: *Famous First Facts.*

47. **How often can Halley's Comet be sighted?**
   ANSWER: Once every 77 years.
   SOURCE: *World Book Encyclopedia*; 1973, Vol. 9.

48. **When is Diana Ross's birthday?**
   ANSWER: She was born on March 26, 1944 in Detroit,
      Michigan.
   SOURCE: *Who's Who in Rock.*

49. **Why are leaves green?**
   ANSWER: Leaves are the main photosynthetic, or food manu-
      facturing organs of plants. They are green because chloro-
      phyll is green and chlorophyll is the major photosynthetic
      pigment.
   SOURCE: *Encyclopedia Americana*; 1973, Vol. 17.

50. **What is the definition of "curd"?**
   ANSWER: Curd is the solid product obtained by the coagula-
      tion (curdling) of milk.
   SOURCE: *Young People's Science Dictionary.*

Inventions

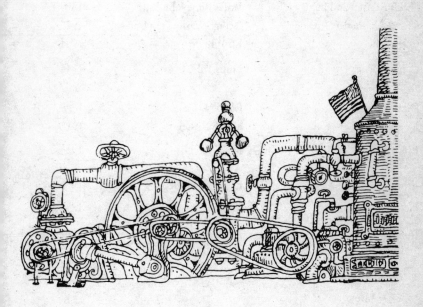

From tapemeasures to TVs, the many gadgets people use had to be invented by someone. Many fascinating facts can be found among the inventors and inventions.

Inventions A-Z

INVENTION	INVENTOR	YEAR PATENTED
Airplane with motor ("Flying Machine")	Orville Wright; Wilbur Wright	1906
Aspirin ("Acetylsalicylic Acid")	Hermann Dresser; Felix Hoffman	1889
Ball point pen	John J. Loud	1888
"Cash Register and Indicator"	James Ritty; John Ritty	1879
Cosmetics (modern)	George Washington Carver	1925
Cotton gin	Eli Whitney	1794
Cylinder lock (Door lock)	Linus Yale, Jr.	1844
Diesel Engine	Rudolf Diesel	1898
Dresser Trunk	Lillian Russel	1912
Electric Razor ("Shaving Implement")	Jacob Schick	1928
Frozen Foods (packaged)	Clarence Birdseye	1930
Icemaking Machine	John Gorrie	1851
Ironing Board	Sarah Boone	1892

INVENTION	INVENTOR	YEAR PATENTED
Laser	Arthur L. Schawlow Charles H. Townes	1960
"Life Raft"	Frederick S. Allen	1881
Mason Jar ("Improvement in Screw Neck Bottles")	John L. Mason	1858
Matches (friction)	Alonso D. Phillips	1836
"Microphone"	Emile Berliner	1880
Motion Picture Projector	Thomas A. Edison	1892
"Motor Carriage"	Henry Ford	1901
Navigable Balloon	J. Etienne; J. Montgolfier	1783
Nuclear Reactor	Enrico Fermi Leo Szilard	1955
Nylon	Wallace H. Carothers	1937
Phonograph	Thomas A. Edison	1877
Pasteurization	Louis Pasteur	1873
Refrigeration	Jacob Perkins	1834
Revolver	Samuel Colt	1836
Rocket Engine	Robert H. Goddard	1914

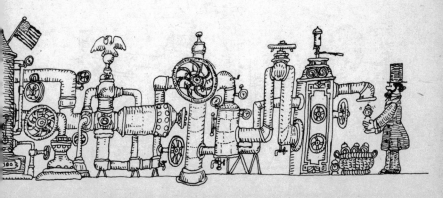

INVENTION	INVENTOR	YEAR PATENTED
Safety Pin	Walter Hunt	1849
Sewing Machine	Elias Howe, Jr.	1846
"Speaking Telegraph"	Thomas A. Edison	1892
Steamboat	Robert Fulton	1811
Stethoscope	William Ford	1882
Suspenders	Samuel Clemens (Mark Twain)	1871
Tape Measure	Alvin J. Fellows	1868
Telegraph Signs	Samuel F. B. Morse	1840
Telephone	Alexander Graham Bell	1876
Television	Philo T. Farnsworth	1930
Typewriter	C. Latham Sholes; Carlos Glidden; Samuel W. Soule	1868
Vacuum Cleaner	Ives W. McGaffey	1869
Videotape Recorder	Charles P. Ginsburg; Shelby Anderson, Jr.; Ray M. Dolby	1960
Vulcanized Rubber	Charles Goodyear	1844
Washing Machine	Chester Stone	1827
Wireless Telegraph	Guglielmo Marconi	1896
Zipper	Whitcomb Judson	1893

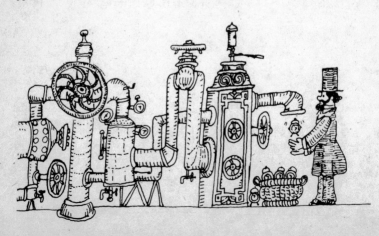

Money

Whether it's an allowance, or a job to earn it, money is a subject of interest to most kids. In this chapter you can learn about money from around the world, find out how much a half a yard is, and learn about some of the different forms of money.

Paper Money

- The Chinese were the first to use paper as money. They introduced paper money in the 8th century A.D.
- Plates for the first paper money printed in the U.S. were designed and engraved by Paul Revere in 1775.
- Washington, D.C. is the only place in the United States where paper money is printed.
- U.S. dollar bills are made of linen and cotton woven with red and blue threads.
- The average life span of a $1 bill is 14 months. The average life span of a $5 bill is 2 years. Fiftys and $100 bills usually last 5 years.
- Sixty percent of the paper currency printed in the U.S. is in $1 bills.
- The U.S. Treasury keeps a record of every bill ever printed. They do this by keeping a list of all serial numbers.
- The first female pictured on U.S. paper currency was Martha Washington who appeared on the 1886 one dollar bill.
- Each U.S. bill has a portrait of a president or historical American.
- The back side of each U.S. bill pictures an event in American history or a government building.
- The serial number of each U.S. bill is printed twice.
- The dates of each U.S. bill tell the year the bill was designed.

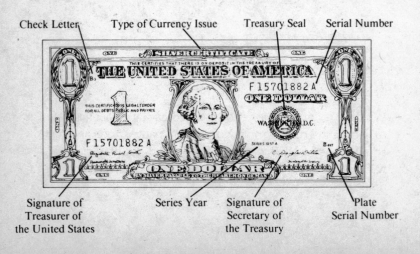

Check Letter   Type of Currency Issue   Treasury Seal   Serial Number

Signature of Treasurer of the United States   Series Year   Signature of Secretary of the Treasury   Plate Serial Number

Coins

• The ancient Lydians were the first to use coins as money. They began the practice in 1700 B.C. (Lydia was a country in what is Turkey today.)

• The first dollar widely used in colonial America was a Dutch coin bearing the likeness of a lion. It was brought to America by Dutch settlers in 1620.

• The first U.S. mint was established by George Washington. Washington contributed his own household silver candlesticks and dishes to be melted down into coins because of a silver shortage.

• The first American common coin to have a president's portrait was the Lincoln penny. In 1909 it was issued to commemorate the 100th anniversary of President Abraham Lincoln's birth.

• The first nickels were minted in 1866. Prior to that time, 5-cent coins were called half dimes and were made of silver.

• The design of any U.S. coin may not be changed more often than 25 years.

• The largest mint in the world is in Philadelphia, Pennsylvania.

• The largest U.S. coin is the Eisenhower dollar.

• All American coins are marked with "In God We Trust" and "E Pluribus Unum." The motto means "One out of many," thought to be a reference to the unity of the states. They are also marked with the following:

    Date of Issue

    U.S.A.

    Designer's initials

    Mint marking

      D for Denver

      S for San Francisco

      P or no mark for Philadelphia

Money Around the World

Basic Units of Money in 20 Countries

COUNTRY	UNIT	COUNTRY	UNIT
Austria	schilling	Jordan	dinar
Brazil	cruzeiro	Laos	kip
Canada	dollar	Mexico	peso
Denmark	krone	Morocco	dirham
France	franc	Netherlands	guilder
Great Britain	pound	Portugal	escudo
Greece	drachma	Russia	ruble
India	rupee	Spain	peseta
Italy	lira	West Germany	deutsche mark
Japan	yen	Zambia	kwacha

Forms of Money

Bonds are loans of money to governments or private companies.
That money is returned to the bondholder with interest, after a
certain amount of time.
Checks are like letters to the bank. They tell the bank to give
some of your money to someone as payment.

Credit cards are used by people who want to pay for something at a later time. The card is an identification card which is shown to the seller. The owner of the card signs a sales slip and usually receives the bill for his or her purchase in the mail.

Money orders are issued by the U.S. Post Office. They can be bought for a small fee. They are most often used by people without checking accounts who want to send money safely through the mail. Money orders can be cashed at any U.S. Post Office.

Stocks are shares in a large company. When the company makes money the stockholder makes money.

Money Talk

The following are money terms and what they mean.

Almighty dollar—This phrase was first used by writer, Washington Irving, in 1836 when he wrote "the almighty dollar, that great object of universal devotion throughout our land."

Bearish—Falling prices, particularly in the stock market. Bears are known to slap their enemies down.

Bill—A word for paper money.

Bullish—Rising prices, particularly in the stock market. Bulls are known to toss their enemies up.

Hush money—Money paid to keep someone quiet.

Kitty—A sum of money collected from a group of people to be used for a certain purpose.

Mad money—Extra money to be used frivolously.

Moneybags—A person with a great deal of money.

Money talks—Money influences people.

Piggybank—First named after the clay called pygg from which early Americans made coin banks. Later these clay coin banks were made into the shape of pigs.

Smart money—Money wisely invested.

Two bits—The first American silver dollar was modeled after the Spanish "piece of eight." When used, this silver dollar was often broken off into two bits ($.25) or four bits ($.50).

Worth his salt—The Romans once paid their soldiers' salaries in salt. Today this term means a person is worth one's wages.

Money Slang

Money — bills, bread, dough, green, lettuce

$1 — ace, bean, buck, one-spot, single

$5 — fin, fiver

$10 — sawbuck, ten-spot

$20 — double sawbuck

$50 — half a yard

$100 — benji, C-note, yard

$500 — five bills, five Cs, half a G

$1000 — a grand, a G, a large

Money Places to Visit

Chicago Mercantile Exchange

30 South Wacker Drive
Chicago, Illinois 60606
The visitors gallery is open to the public from 7:15 A.M. to 3:15 P.M. Visitors can see the action on the trading floor where commodities (i.e., grains, metals, and livestock) are bought and sold. Guided tours are available by reservation. The guides explain the workings of the commodities exchange.

Denver Mint

320 West Colfax
Denver, Colorado 80204
The mint conducts a 20-minute tour Monday through Friday, 8:30 A.M. to 3:00 P.M. There is an exhibit of coins and a bal-cony from which visitors may look down on moneymaking operations.

Fort Knox

Fort Knox, Kentucky 40121
Visitors are not allowed inside this high security building. They may tour the nearby army base and view the large granite, steel, and concrete building which holds a large amount of the U.S. government's gold. Approximately 150 million ounces of gold are stored in this depository.

Homestake Mine

Box 875
Lead, South Dakota 57754
This is a privately owned gold mine which conducts a 1¼-hour walking tour for the pub-

lic. Visitors can view the surface workings of the mine and the final processing of gold.

New York Stock Exchange
20 Broad Street
New York, New York 10005
Visitors are allowed in the observation gallery from 10:00 A.M. to 3:00 P.M. Monday through Friday to watch the activities of trading stocks. A guide is available to explain how to read the ticker tape.

Philadelphia Mint
5th and Arch Streets
Philadelphia, Pennsylvania 19106
Visitors are allowed to take self-guided tours on weekdays from 9:00 A.M. to 4:30 P.M. Coin exhibits are on display and coin production can be viewed.

San Francisco Mint
55 Mint Street
San Francisco, California 94175
Visitors may not view coin production at this mint. However, visitors are offered a movie, which tells the story of the San Francisco mint, and a museum, which features a replica of the gold rush days.

Sutter's Mill and Marshall Gold Discovery State Historical Park
P.O. Box 265
Coloma, California 95613
Visitors may take a self-guided tour through the museum which contains a replica of the original mill where gold was first discovered in the U.S. There are dioramas which show the many uses of gold throughout history.

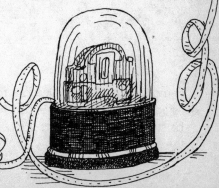

Museums

THE MUSEUM OF MUSEUMS

Famous and offbeat collections found in the United States are listed in this chapter. Whether your interest is baseball cards or stuffed animals, there's a museum for you.

Must-See U.S. Museum Collections

Aircraft

National Air and Space
  Museum
Independence Ave. (4th & 7th
  St.) SW
Washington, D.C. 20560

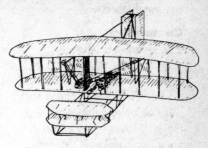

This museum features aircraft ranging from the Wright brothers' original plane and Lindbergh's *Spirit of St. Louis*, to World War II fighter planes and the *Apollo II* spacecraft. People's early interest in flight can be viewed in the collection of Chinese kites and balloons.

Automobiles

Henry Ford Museum
20900 Oakwood Boulevard
Dearborn, Michigan 41821

This museum is famous for its collection of automobiles. There are more than 200 old cars, including Henry Ford's first car, the 1907 Rolls Royce Silver Ghost, and the 1914 Detroit Electric.

Baseball Cards

Metropolitan Museum of Art
5th Ave. and 80th St.
New York, New York 10028

The Print Room of this museum houses the world-famous Burdick collection of baseball and tobacco cards. It is the largest and most extensive collection of baseball cards available for viewing in the U.S.

Buffalo Bill Memorabilia

Buffalo Bill Historical Center
P.O. Box 1000
Cody, Wyoming 82414

The personal items of Buffalo Bill Cody including guns, saddles, clothing, and trophies can be found in this museum. In addition, artifacts from his traveling show, among them Annie Oakley's fringed rawhide outfit, are on display here.

Coal Mining Machinery

Museum of Science and
  Industry
57th St. and Lake Shore Dr.
Chicago, Illinois 60637

A full-sized reproduction of a coal mine is on display here. Visitors enter the mine in a real mine hoist. A guided tour explains the machinery and technology used in modern mining methods.

Computers

The Computer Museum
300 Congress St.
Boston, Massachusetts 01752
Computers made of tinker toys, huge obsolete computers, and the very latest home computers are all on display at this museum. It is a one-of-a-kind collection that takes both a serious and humorous look at computers.

Circus Wagons

Circus World Museum
426 Water St.
Baraboo, Wisconsin 53913
Over 100 circus wagons are on display in this museum. It is the world's largest collection of circus wagons and is situated on land once owned by the Ringling Brothers. Circus parades, aerial arts, and clown shows are also featured at this museum.

Dinosaurs

Carnegie Museum of Natural History
Carnegie Institute
4400 Forbes Ave.
Pittsburgh, Pennsylvania 15213
The museum's Dinosaur Hall houses one of the world's best exhibits devoted to dinosaurs. Mounted dinosaurs include the finest allosaurus ever found, a protoceratops with its egg, and a Tyrannosaurus rex.

Dog Artwork

The Dog Museum
New York Life Insurance Bldg.
51 Madison Ave. (26th & 27th St.)
New York, New York 10010
Dogs have been prominent in artwork for centuries, from early cave paintings to modern works. This exhibit is devoted entirely to dogs and includes bronze sculptures, 18th-century paintings, and photographs.

Dolls
Margaret Woodbury Strong
   Museum
One Manhattan Square
Rochester, New York 14607
More than 19,000 dolls of every type and fashion from all over the world are on display here. There are also thousands of doll houses, miniature houses, trains and toys to delight kids and grown-ups alike.

First Ladies' Gowns
National Museum of American
   History
Constitution Ave. (12th &
   14th St.) NW
Washington, D.C. 20560
Every U.S. president's wife is featured in this exhibit. Life-size replicas of the women dressed in their inaugural gowns are displayed in period settings.

Flags
National Museum of American
   History
Constitution Ave. (12th &
   14th St.) NW
Washington, D.C. 20560
Among the many flags displayed is the original "Old Glory" which inspired Francis Scott Key to write the words for the U.S. national anthem, "The Star-Spangled Banner."

Kids
Children's Museum
P.O. Box 3000
Worth Meridian
Indianapolis, Indiana 46206
This is the largest children's museum in the world. There are more than 75,000 objects kids can touch or handle. Visitors can sit at the wheel of a racing car or ride an 80-year-old merry-go-round.

Mechanical Music
Musical Museum
Main St.
Deansboro, New York 13328
The world's largest collection of mechanical music machines is housed in this 17-room museum. Nickleodeons, organ grinders, and rice organs are displayed, and classical and ragtime are among the musical styles they play.

Oceans
Planet Ocean
3975 Richenbachen Causeway
Miami, Florida 33149
At this museum you can see a
real iceberg, step into a hurricane, and look through the
jaws of a shark. Action exhibits
based on the ocean and its animals are displayed here.

Police Memorabilia
New York City Police Acad-
    emy Museum
235 East 20th St.
New York, New York 10003
Exhibits here include police
uniforms and equipment, as
well as weapons captured by
police from famed gangster Al
Capone and other criminals.

Seagoing Vessels
Mystic Seaport Museum
Greenmanville Ave.
Mystic, Connecticut 06355
This museum is devoted to
American sailors and sailing.
On exhibit are whaling ships,
carved figureheads, anchors,
harpoons, and all types of ob-
jects related to the shipping and
whaling trade.

Stuffed Animals
Foster's Bighorn
143 Main Street
Rio Vista, California 94571
Known as the world's largest
"inert zoo," this collection of
stuffed animals includes exam-
ples of rare and extinct species.
This huge collection is worth
over 3 million dollars.

Trains

National Museum of Transport
3015 Barrett Station Rd.
Saint Louis, Missouri 63122
Classic steam locomotives, early diesels, Pullman sleeping cars, lavish dining cars, cabooses, and early refrigerated cars are some of the sights for train lovers to see at this museum.

Trolleys

Seashore Trolley Museum
Drawer A
Log Cabin Rd.
Kennebunkport, Maine 04046
One of the world's most complete collections of street and railway vehicles can be seen here. Many are on display, but some are in service on the museum's demonstration railway and road.

Music

Rock, Pop, Reggae, Folk, Country, Jazz, Swing. If you like music, these pages will "sing" with things you'll want to know.

Music Trivia

1. **What is the most popular Christian hymn in the U.S.?**
   ANSWER: "Abide With Me."
2. **What is the most popular musical instrument in the U.S.?**
   ANSWER: More Americans play the piano than any other instrument.
3. **What composer has written the most million-selling singles in pop music?**
   ANSWER: Paul McCartney.
4. **What is the most frequently sung song in the world?**
   ANSWER: "Happy Birthday to You" written by the American sisters Patty and Mildred Hill in 1893.
5. **Who is the person generally credited with the first solo recital?**
   ANSWER: Franz Liszt, a piano virtuoso who lived in Hungary in the 1800s.
6. **Who won the most Grammy Awards (given for artistic achievement in the recording field) in one year?**
   ANSWER: Michael Jackson, who won 8 for the year 1983.
7. **Who was the first recording artist to win a gold record?**
   ANSWER: Perry Como in 1958 for his song "Catch A Falling Star."
8. **Who is the best-selling classical pianist in recording history?**
   ANSWER: Polish-born Arthur Rubinstein, who first played in the U.S. in 1906. He has become one of the most widely-loved U.S. concert pianists selling more than 10 million of his 200 recordings.
9. **What is the biggest and most powerful musical instrument?**
   ANSWER: The pipe organ. The largest pipe organ on record is the Auditorium Organ in Atlantic City, New Jersey, which has 33,112 pipes and the volume of 25 brass bands.
10. **What orchestra has given more concerts than any other in the world?**
    ANSWER: The New York Philharmonic began playing in 1842. In 1982 it played its 10,000th concert and has performed over a thousand more since then.
11. **Who was the most famous violin maker in history?**
    ANSWER: Antonio Stradivarius (1644–1737) of Italy. No one has been able to duplicate the sound of his violins. It is not

known whether his formula for varnish, the sap applied to the wood, or the wood itself is the secret to his violins. Today, a Stradivarius violin is worth over $450,000.

12. **What was the first opera every composed?**
ANSWER: *Dafne* by Jacopo Peri of Florence, Italy in 1597.

13. **What instrument do most kids in most marching bands want to play?**
ANSWER: The drums.

14. **Where is the capital of jazz in the United States?**
ANSWER: New Orleans, Louisiana.

15. **What was the first Broadway musical written and produced by blacks?**
ANSWER: *Shuffle Along* by Eubie Blake and Nobel Sissle in 1921.

16. **What music is played when the president of the U.S. appears in public?**
ANSWER: "Hail to the Chief."

17. **What was the first music video nominated for an Academy Award (given for excellence in motion pictures)?**
ANSWER: *Thriller* by Michael Jackson.

18. **Who was the most successful music group ever?**
ANSWER: The Beatles sold over a hundred million singles and a hundred million albums.

19. **What was the first television station to feature video music exclusively?**
ANSWER: Music Television (MTV) began in 1981 as a 24-hour, seven-day-a-week rock channel playing video songs only.

20. **What was the greatest selling classical record?**
ANSWER: *Switched-on Bach* by Walter Carlos (1968) featuring many of Bach's best known works played on the Moog Synthesizer.

21. **Is there such a thing as a one-man orchestra?**
ANSWER: Yes, a "Symphonytron" which is an electronic instrument, allows a player to perform a symphony written for many instruments on a single machine.

Gold Record Chart

This is a list of the number of records that must be sold to win a gold record in countries around the world.

COUNTRY	NUMBER OF SINGLES	COUNTRY	NUMBER OF SINGLES
Australia	50,000	Italy	1,000,000
Austria	100,000	The Netherlands	100,000
Canada	75,000	Poland	250,000
Denmark	50,000	Spain	100,000
Finland	10,000	Sweden	100,000
France	500,000	United Kingdom	500,000
Hungary	100,000	U.S.A.	1,000,000
Ireland	100,000	West Germany	1,000,000

Musical Notes

Five Musicians Who Influenced Popular Music

Bill Haley and His Comets—Rock 'n' Roll

Woody Guthrie—Folk Music

Ray Charles—Rhythm and Blues

Dave Brubeck—Modern Progressive Jazz

Bob Marley—Reggae Music

Five Funny Song Titles

"The Purple People Eater"—1958

"Does Your Chewing Gum Lose Its Flavor on the Bedpost Overnight?"—1961

"The Monster Mash"—1962

"Itsy Bitsy Teenie Weenie Yellow Polka Dot Bikini"—1960

"A Boy Named Sue"—1968

Five Grammy Award-Winning "Records of the Year"

1980 "Sailing," sung by Christopher Cross

1981 "Bette Davis Eyes," sung by Kim Carnes

1982 "Rosanna," sung by Toto

1983 "Beat It," sung by Michael Jackson

1984 "What's Love Got to Do With It," sung by Tina Turner

Five Musical Groups with Food Names

The Electric Prunes
Meat Loaf
The Flying Burrito Brothers
The Strawberry Alarm Clock
Vanilla Fudge

Top Five Performers with the Most Pop Hits (1953–1983)

Elvis Presley
The Beatles
James Brown
Pat Boone
Fats Domino

Five Kings of Music

"The King"—Elvis Presley
"King of Swing"—Benny Goodman
"King of Ragtime"—Scott Joplin
"King of Mountain Music"—Roy Acuff
"King of the Twelve-String Guitar"—Leadbelly (Huddie Ledbetter)

Kids' Five Favorite Broadway Musicals

1. Annie
2. Grease
3. Oklahoma
4. Oliver
5. West Side Story

Five Queens of Music

"Queen of Soul"—Aretha Franklin
"Queen of the Blues"—Dinah Washington
"Queen of Country Music"—Mother Maybelle Carter
"Queen of Folk Music"—Joan Baez
"Queen of Rock"—Janis Joplin

Five Musical Groups with Animal Names

The Beatles
The Byrds
The Eagles
The Monkees
The Turtles

Five Firsts in Rock 'n' Roll

- The first to use the term rock 'n' roll was Alan Freed, a disc jockey from Cleveland. In 1952 he changed the name of his radio show to "Morning Rock 'n' Roll House Party."
- The first national rock 'n' roll hit was "Sh-Boom (Life Would Be A Dream)" by the Chords. It was recorded in 1954.
- The first rock film was *Blackboard Jungle*. This 1955 movie featured the hit song "Rock Around the Clock" by Bill Haley and His Comets.
- The first to win a Gold Record for a rock 'n' roll single was Elvis Presley for his 1958 hit "Hard Headed Woman."
- The first Broadway rock musical was *Hair* which opened in 1968.

Five Kinds of Songs

Aria—A song with an instrumental accompaniment. Arias appear most commonly in operas.

Ballad—A folk song that tells a story.

Carol—A traditional song heard at Christmastime or on other holidays.

Round/Canon—A song in which all parts and voices have the same melody, each starting at a different time (e.g., "Row Row Row Your Boat . . .").

Shanty—A song sung by sailors in earlier times to help them keep a rhythm as they worked.

Five Song Titles That Became Popular Sayings

"The Times They Are A-Changing'," Bob Dylan

"Give Peace A Chance," John Lennon and Paul McCartney

"Say It Loud 'I'm Black and I'm Proud'," James Brown

"You Are The Sunshine of My Life," Stevie Wonder

"I Can't Get No Satisfaction," Mick Jagger and Keith Richards

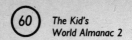

Five Kinds of Rock Music

MUSIC	EXAMPLES OF MUSICIANS
Heavy Metal (Hard Rock)	Van Halen
New Wave	The Pretenders
Pop Rock	Olivia Newton-John
Punk	The Clash
Country Rock	The Stray Cats

Five Kinds of Jazz Music

MUSIC	EXAMPLES OF MUSICIANS
Boogie Woogie	Jelly Roll Morton
Blues	Bessie Smith
Dixieland	The Preservation Hall Band
Progressive	Miles Davis
Ragtime	Scott Joplin

Five Kinds of Country Music

MUSIC	EXAMPLES OF MUSICIANS
Bluegrass	Bill Monroe
Cajun	Doug Kershaw
Country and Western	Hank Williams
Country Gospel	The Oak Ridge Boys
Western Swing	Bob Wills and the Texas Playboys

Classical Musical Notes

Five Music Professions

A composer writes music.

A conductor directs the performances of a chorus, band or orchestra.

A performer either plays an instrument or works as a solo or group artist.

A teacher works in a school or gives private lessons.

A tuner tunes musical instruments.

Five Forms of Classical Music

Ballet—A story danced to music, usually with scenery and costumes.

Concerto—A work for one or more solo instruments and orchestra.

Opera—A play or story that is sung and acted. An opera is usually staged with costumes, scenery, a chorus, and an orchestra.

Oratorio—A religious story put to music and usually performed by a chorus without scenery and costumes.

Symphony—A long musical composition for orchestra.

Five Great Composers for Young People

Robert Schumann, a German who lived in the 1800s, was one of the first to write piano pieces for children. Among his works are "Album for the Young" and "Scenes from Childhood."

Peter Ilyich Tchaikovsky was a Russian composer who lived from 1840 to 1893. He composed the music for *The Nutcracker*, a ballet loved by children.

Johannes Brahms, 19th-century German composer, wrote a now-famous lullaby, which has been sung by parents to babies for over a hundred years.

Sergei Prokofiev, who lived in Russia from 1891–1953, composed *Peter and the Wolf*, a classic favorite of kids.

Aaron Copeland, a modern American composer, wrote an opera for children to peform entitled *The Second Hurricane*.

Five Notable Music Festivals

The Aspen Festival takes place in Aspen, Colorado every summer. Concerts, recitals, and chamber music are performed.

The Bayreuth Festival is held in Bayreuth, Germany every July and August. The festival is dedicated to the music of Richard Wagner's operas.

The Berkshire Festival, also known as Tanglewood, is held near Lenox, Massachusetts every July and August. Operas, chamber music, and concert performances of the Boston Symphony Orchestra are featured.

The Edinburgh Festival is known for the variety of its music. It presents operas, ballets, and concerts every year from late August into September.

The Salzburg Festival in Salzburg, Austria is dedicated to the music of Mozart although other composers' works are included in the festival. It runs from late July through August every year.

Five Famous National Anthems

• **"God Save the King,"** the royal anthem of Great Britain, is called the "anthem of anthems." Its melody is one of the most popular tunes in the world. Germany, Denmark, Sweden, Switzerland, and the U.S. all have national songs written to its tune. "My Country Tis of Thee" is the American national song which is sung to this melody.

• The national anthem of Austria is considered to be one of the most beautiful. **"Got Erhaltz"** (May God Save) was composed by the great Austrian composer, Joseph Haydn.

• **"The Marseillaise,"** is the national anthem of France. Next to "God Save the King," it is the best-known national anthem. It was written by Claude Joseph de Lisle, a loyal subject of King Louis XVI. However, it was later used against the king as the song of the revolutionaries. In 1795 it became the official anthem of France.

• The words to **"The Star-spangled Banner"** were written by Francis Scott Key in 1814 when he watched the British bomb Fort McHenry near Baltimore. It was not until 117 years later in 1931 that a law was passed making "The Star-spangled Banner" the National Anthem of the U.S.

• The tiny country of Vatican City has an anthem. It is called the **"Marcia Pontificale"** and was composed by Charles Gounod for Pope Pius IX in 1846. It became the official papal anthem in 1949.

The Orchestra

The orchestra is made up of four families of musical instruments. There are usually about 100 instruments in a standard orchestra.

String Instruments

About two-thirds of the orchestra is made up of instruments in the string family. The sounds of these instruments are made by drawing a bow across the strings or by plucking them.

Violin

A four-stringed instrument, it is the smallest instrument in this family. Violins are the largest group of instruments in the orchestra; about thirty-six are in a standard orchestra.

Viola

An instrument like the violin, the viola is only one-seventh larger in size. The tone of the viola is lower than the violin. There are usually eight to ten violas in an orchestra.

Cello

Twice the size of the viola, the cello is held between the knees. Its tone is eight notes lower than the viola and there are usually ten to twelve celli in an orchestra.

Double Bass

The largest stringed instrument, it stands six feet tall. The player stands or sits on a high stool to play it. There are eight to ten in an orchestra.

Harp

The oldest instrument in the string section, the harp is also the only stringed instrument not in the violin family. Instead of four strings it has forty-seven, and it has seven pedals. The harp is not always played in an orchestra.

Woodwind Instruments

These instruments were named because they were originally made of wood and played by blowing wind into them. Today, they are still played in the same manner but many are made of metal rather than of wood. The notes are produced by pressing on the keys of the instrument.

Flute

This instrument is about two feet long and is held horizontally when played. The tones are made by pressing keys with the fingers. There are three in an orchestra.

Piccolo

This instrument is a half-size flute that plays notes higher than the flute. There is one in an orchestra.

Oboe

A two-foot-long instrument, it is held vertically when played. The oboe is a double-reed instrument, meaning it has a mouthpiece made of two pieces of cane wood tied around a small tube. There are three in an orchestra.

English Horn

A kind of oboe, this instrument is five notes lower and is one-and-a-half times the size of an oboe. There is one English horn player in an orchestra.

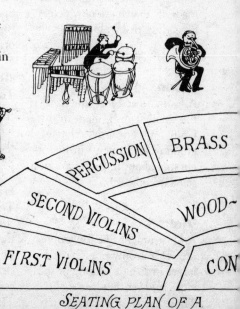

SEATING PLAN OF A

Clarinet

This is a single-reed instrument. There are three in an orchestra.

Bass Clarinet

Twice as large as a clarinet, this instrument plays eight notes lower. It is used occasionally in an orchestra.

Bassoon

An eight-foot-long instrument, it is doubled over to make it easier to handle. There are two in an orchestra.

Double Bassoon/Contra Bassoon

This instrument is sixteen feet long but doubled four times to make it shorter. It plays the lowest notes of the woodwind instruments. There is one double bassoon player in an orchestra.

Brass Instruments

All of the instruments in this family are made of metal. They are blown to make music.

Trumpet

This instrument is played by pressing three valves. The tube of a trumpet is eight feet long but is coiled around so the instrument is shorter and easier to handle. There are four trumpet players in an orchestra.

BRASS

STRING BASSES

WINDS

VIOLAS

UCTOR

CELLOS

HARP

TYPICAL SYMPHONY ORCHESTRA

French Horn

There are three valves in a French horn which are pressed to produce different tones. The tube of this instrument is sixteen feet long and coiled around to make it manageable. There are three French horn players in an orchestra.

Trombone

This instrument has no valves. The tones are produced by moving the slide back and forth while blowing into the instrument. A standard orchestra has three trombones.

Tuba

The heaviest and largest of brass instruments, its mouthpiece covers the mouth of most players. If the tube of this instrument were uncoiled it would stretch five feet. The tone, made by pressing valves, is very low. There is one tuba player in an orchestra.

Percussion Instruments

Drums

Snare drums are 16 inches across, the smallest in the drum family. Bass drums are four times larger than the snare. Kettle drums look like enormous kettles. There are three to four in an orchestra, each producing different tones.

Triangle

The simplest instrument in the orchestra, it is made of steel shaped into a triangle. It tinkles like a bell when struck with a metal rod.

Cymbals

Two brass plates which are clapped together to make a crashing sound.

Gong

A large brass plate four to five feet across, which is hung in place and played with a wooden mallet.

People Who Are Important to the Orchestra

• **The composer** writes the music the orchestra plays. The parts for all the various instruments are written by the composer.

• **The conductor** interprets the music and directs the performance of the orchestra. The conductor must be able to read all the musical parts at once.

• **The concertmaster** is the first violinist and is the lead musician in the orchestra. The concertmaster helps the conductor train and rehearse the musicians in the orchestra.

• **The copyist** makes the music for each member of the orchestra to read.

• **The librarian** is responsible for arranging the chairs, music stands, and music for each member of the orchestra.

• **The manager** makes the arrangements for the performances of the orchestra. A manager schedules performing dates and makes all travel and hotel arrangements for the orchestra when it travels.

Ten Italian Musical Terms

1. **A capella** (ah cah-pel' lah)—Unaccompanied choral singing.
2. **Adagio** (ah-dah' jo)—Slowly.
3. **Allegro** (ah-lay' groh)—Fast and lively.
4. **Crescendo** (creh-shen' doh)—Growing louder.
5. **Decrescendo** (day-creh-shen' doh)—Growing softer.
6. **Forte** (for' tay)—Loud.
7. **Largo** (lar' goh)—Slow.
8. **Legato** (lay-gah' toh)—Smooth and connected. To be played with no interruptions between notes.

9. *Staccato* (stah-cah' toh)—Sharply detached, one note from another.

10. **Tutti** (toot' ee)—The part of a composition in which all the instruments or voices perform together.

Milestones in Recording History

1877   Thomas Alva Edison of Menlo Park, New Jersey, first recorded sound on December 6th. The tune he recorded was "Mary Had a Little Lamb."

1888   The first popular artist to make a recording was 12-year-old Josef Hoffman, a pianist. He recorded a brief passage at the Edison Laboratories in New Jersey.

1903   The first "unbreakable" record was made by Nicole Freres. He made it out of cardboard covered with shellac.

1927   The first record changer was introduced by The Victor Talking Machine Company of New Jersey.

1936   Billboard published the first pop record sales chart.

1949   The first 45-rpm record was made by RCA.

1953   The first rock 'n' roll song made the Billboard charts. The song was "Crazy Man Crazy" sung by Bill Haley and His Comets.

1954   Les Paul built the first multi-track (8-track) tape recorder. He also discovered the technique of echo or delay which revolutionized the sound of recording.

1954   Tape cartridges were invented by George Eash, a Los Angeles engineer.

1958   Stero LPs were first marketed in the U.S.

1959   The first album sold without the name of the artist on the front or back of the album cover was For LP Fans Only by Elvis Presley.

Native Instruments Around the World

INSTRUMENT	COUNTRY OF ORIGIN	INSTRUMENT	COUNTRY OF ORIGIN
1. Alpenhorn	Switzerland	6. Marimba	Guatemala
2. Bagpipe	Scotland	7. Sitar	India
3. Balalaika	Russia	8. Spike Fiddle	Thailand
4. Cimbalon	Hungary	9. Steel Drums	West Indies
5. Gusla	Yugoslavia	10. Trompong	Bali

Presidents of the U.S.

There have been forty men who have served as president of the United States. The highlights of their terms of office, their sporting interests, and little known facts about these men are included in this chapter.

Presidential Achievements

NAME AND YEARS IN OFFICE	HIGHLIGHTS OF ADMINISTRATION
1. George Washington 1789–1793 1793–1797	Created Department of Foreign Affairs, national bank, patent laws, Post Office, Treasury Post Office and the Treasury; Bank of U.S. Chartered.
2. John Adams 1797–1801	Established the Library of Congress, Marine Corps, Navy, and public health services.
3. Thomas Jefferson 1801–1805 1805–1809	Purchased Louisiana Territory; authorized the Lewis and Clark expedition; ended African slave import, established Army Corps of Engineers.
4. James Madison 1809–1813 1813–1817	Issued first war bonds; U.S. defeated England in War of 1812.
5. James Monroe 1817–1821 1821–1825	Purchased Florida; issued Monroe Doctrine (a warning to Europe to stop colonizing America); Missouri Compromise (slave state issue).
6. John Quincy Adams 1825–1829	Opened western America for settlement with the building of canals, highways, and railroads.
7. Andrew Jackson 1829–1833 1833–1837	Introduced "spoils system" by which friends were awarded government jobs; reopened U.S. trade with West Indies.
8. Martin van Buren 1837–1841	Created independent treasury system to deal with economic panic of 1837.
9. William Henry Harrison 1841	Died a month after taking office.
10. John Tyler 1841–1845	Annexed Texas; established uniform election day; signed treaty with China.
11. James Knox Polk 1845–1849	Established the Department of the Interior; purchased California, New Mexico, Arizona, Nevada, Utah and parts of Colorado; settled Oregon boundary dispute with Great Britain.
12. Zachary Taylor 1849–1850	Signed a treaty with Hawaiian Islands; Compromise of 1850 (slave state issue); died after 16 months in office.

NAME AND YEARS IN OFFICE	HIGHLIGHTS OF ADMINISTRATION
13. Millard Fillmore 1850–1853	Sent Commodore Perry to Japan to open trade with U.S.; Fugitive Slave Law enacted (runaway slaves must be returned to owners).
14. Franklin Pierce 1853–1857	Signed treaty with Japan; Gadsden Purchase of Mexico border land; Kansas Nebraska Act (state choice on slavery issue).
15. James Buchanan 1857–1861	Dred Scott decision by Supreme Court deprived Congress of the right to end slavery; South Carolina seceded from the U.S.
16. Abraham Lincoln 1861–1865	Issued Emancipation Proclamation which freed slaves; Civil War fought; established Department of Agriculture; proclaimed Thanksgiving Day as national holiday; assassinated.
17. Andrew Jackson 1865–1869	Purchased Alaska; 14th Amendment passed to establish the rights of U.S. citizens.
18. Ulysses S. Grant 1869–1873 1873–1877	Created Department of Justice; transcontinental railroad completed; financial panic, political scandals.
19. Rutherford B. Hayes 1877–1881	Women allowed to practice law before the Supreme Court; the last Federal troops were withdrawn from the South.
20. James A. Garfield 1881	Established American Red Cross; assassinated after 199 days in office.
21. Chester A. Arthur 1881–1885	Signed treaty with Korea; civil service reform act passed; standard time adopted.
22. Grover Cleveland 1885–1889 and 24. 1893–1897	Interstate Commerce Commission established; gold standard maintained; western U.S. homesteaded.
23. Benjamin Harrison 1889–1893	Sherman Antitrust Act passed, which broke up business monopolies. Six states entered U.S.: Washington, Idaho, Montana, Wyoming, North Dakota and South Dakota.
25. William McKinley 1897–1901	Spanish-American War won, whereby U.S. acquired Philippines, Puerto Rico, and Guam from Spain; Hawaii annexed by U.S.; assassinated.

NAME AND YEARS IN OFFICE	HIGHLIGHTS OF ADMINISTRATION
26. **Theodore Roosevelt** 1901–1905 1905–1909	Created Department of Commerce and Labor; Pure Food and Drug Act and Meat Inspection Act passed to protect consumers; Panama Canal Zone leased to U.S. for use of the canal.
27. **William Howard Taft** 1909–1913	Established postal banks and parcel post; Congress given power to tax citizen incomes.
28. **Woodrow Wilson** 1913–1917 1917–1921	Purchased Danish West Indies (now U.S. Virgin Islands); FTC and Federal Reserve System created; 19th Amendment (women's voting rights) passed; World War I began.
29. **Warren G. Harding** 1921–1923	Created Bureau of the Budget; first immigration quota passed; political scandals.
30. **Calvin Coolidge** 1923–1925 1925–1929	Created the Foreign Service and U.S. Radio Commission; U.S. citizenship granted to American Indians.
31. **Herbert C. Hoover** 1929–1933	Created Veterans Administration; adopted "Star-Spangled Banner" as the National Anthem; economic depression.
32. **Franklin D. Roosevelt** 1933–1937 1937–1941 1941–1945	Brought U.S. out of Great Depression; U.S. entered WW II; Government reform and expansion through programs such as the Social Security Act and Minimum Wage Laws.
33. **Harry S. Truman** 1945–1949 1949–1953	U.S. dropped atom bomb on Japan; WW II ended; Korean War began; North Atlantic Treaty Organization (NATO) established; Truman Doctrine (halted Russian expansion into Europe and Asia).
34. **Dwight D. Eisenhower** 1953–1957 1957–1961	Korean War ended; racial integration of schools enforced; created National Aeronautics and Space Administration (NASA) which launched first U.S. satellites.
35. **John F. Kennedy** 1961–1963	Created Peace Corps; established "hotline" (direct telephone line between Soviet and U.S. leaders); forced Russia to remove missiles from Cuba; first man launched into space; assassinated.
36. **Lyndon B. Johnson** 1963–1965 1965–1969	Escalated U.S. involvement in Viet Nam; passed legislation on civil rights and tax reduction; established anti-poverty and conservation programs.

NAME AND YEARS IN OFFICE	**HIGHLIGHTS OF ADMINISTRATION**
37. **Richard M. Nixon** 1969–1972 1972–1974	First man on the moon; established relations with the Peoples Republic of China; ended Viet Nam War; political scandal and resignation from office of president.
38. **Gerald R. Ford** 1974–1977	President Nixon pardoned; passed Federal Campaign Reform Act; proposed statehood for Puerto Rico.
39. **James E. Carter** 1977–1981	Pardoned Viet Nam draft resisters; led negotiations for peace in the Middle East; signed treaty which gave the Panama Canal back to Panama in the year 2000.
40. **Ronald W. Reagan** 1981–1984 1984–	Lifted controls on oil pricing; instituted a freeze on hiring new government employees; ordered U.S. invasion of Grenada.

Singular Facts About U.S. Presidents

Arrested President Ulysses S. Grant was stopped by a policeman while he was driving his carriage through Washington, D.C. He was issued a ticket for speeding. Rather than appear for a court trial, Grant paid a fine of $20.

Bachelor President James Buchanan was the first bachelor elected to the presidency. He never married and was known as the bachelor president. His niece, Jane Lane, served as "first lady" during his administration.

Gourmet President Thomas Jefferson was an excellent cook and food lover. He is credited with introducing ice cream, waffles and spaghetti to America.

Heaviest President William Taft was 6 feet tall and weighed between 300 and 350 pounds.

Horse at the White House President Zachary Taylor, a war hero, brought his favorite horse, "Whitey," with him when he moved into the White House. The horse was allowed to graze and run on the White House lawn.

Impeached	President Andrew Johnson was the only president to be impeached. He was later acquitted, by one vote, of the charges of usurping the law, corrupt use of the veto power, interference at elections and misdemeanors. He served out the rest of his term.
Inaugurated in 2 Cities	On April 30, 1743, President George Washington was inaugurated in New York City, the nation's first capital. He took his second oath of office in Philadelphia, Pennsylvania, the second U.S. capital city. He was the only president inaugurated in two different cities.
Inventor	President Abraham Lincoln was the only U.S. president to patent an invention. He received patent 6469 for a floatable device to allow steamboats to pass over shallow waters. He was awarded the patent in 1849, twelve years before he was elected president.
Longest Lived	President John Adams was the president who lived the longest. He died on July 4, 1826 at the age of 90. He became president when he was 61 years old, served for 4 years, and lived for 25 years after his term.
Longest Term of Office	President Franklin D. Roosevelt was the only president to be elected 4 times. He served for 12 years and 39 days and died while still in office. In 1951 a law was passed to limit the office of president to two terms.
Married in the White House	President Grover Cleveland was the only president to be married in the White House. When elected, he was a bachelor, but on June 2, 1886, he married Frances Folson at a ceremony which took place in the White House.
Most Children	President John Tyler had more children than any other U.S. president. His first child, Mary, was born in 1815. His last child, Pearl, was born in 1860. All together Tyler sired fifteen children. His first wife, Letitia Christian, bore eight children. After her death, his second wife, Julia Gardiner, gave birth to seven more children.
Name on the Moon	President Richard Nixon is the only president whose name is inscribed on a plaque on the moon. The plaque was left on the moon by the Apollo II astronauts.
Oldest Inaugurated	President Ronald Reagan was the oldest person to be elected president. He was 69 years, 349 days old when he took the oath of office. He was reelected at age 74.
Resigned	President Richard Nixon was the only president to resign from office. During his second term, he bowed to the pressures of the nation and Congress to resign or face impeachment because of the "Watergate" scandal. His resignation officially took place at noon on August 9, 1974. Vice-President Gerald Ford became the next president.

Shortest Term of Office	President William H. Harrison died after serving only 32 days as President. He caught a chill during his inaugural ceremonies and later died of pneumonia.
Smallest	President James Madison was the shortest man to serve as President. He was 5 feet, 4 inches tall and weighed about 100 pounds.
Sworn in by Father	The only president to be sworn into office by his father was Calvin Coolidge. Upon the sudden death of President Harding, the then vice-president took the oath of office before his father, John, a notary public. The event took place at their home in Plymouth, Vermont at 2:47 A.M. on August 3, 1923.
Tallest	President Abraham Lincoln was a towering 6-foot, 4-inch man. He was the tallest U.S. president.
Unknown	The only man to be U.S. president for a day was David Rice Atchison. There was no official president for one day after President Polk's term expired and President Taylor's began. For religious reasons, Taylor would not be sworn in on a Sunday. So, from noon on Sunday, March 4 until noon on Monday, March 5, 1849, Atchison, the president of the Senate, was the head of state.
Youngest	President Theodore Roosevelt was the youngest person to serve as president. When President McKinley was assassinated, Vice-President Roosevelt took the oath of office. He was 42 years and 10 months old.
Youngest Elected	The youngest person to be elected to the presidency was John F. Kennedy. He was 43 years and 236 days old when he took the oath of office.

Favorite Sports of the Presidents

PRESIDENT	FAVORITE SPORT(S)
George Washington	Billiards, canoeing, cockfighting, exploring, fishing, horse racing, hunting, riding.
John Adams	Horseback riding, hunting, ice skating, swimming, townball (early version of baseball).
Thomas Jefferson	Fishing, horse racing, horseback riding, running, swimming, walking.
James Madison	Walking.
James Monroe	Fishing, horseback riding, hunting, swimming.
John Quincy Adams	Billiards, horse racing, horseback riding, swimming, walking.
Andrew Jackson	Cockfighting, horse racing, horseback riding. (He kept a stable of thoroughbreds on the White House lawn.)
Martin Van Buren	Horseback riding, walking.
William Henry Harrison	Horseback riding.
John Tyler	Horseback riding, marbles.
James Polk	None, he was sickly. At age 14 he had a serious operation on his stomach.
Zachary Taylor	Horseback riding, hunting, swimming.
Millard Fillmore	None, he was forbade participation in sports because he had to work 12 to 15 hours a day as a weaver helping his father.
Franklin Pierce	Swimming, walking.
James Buchanan	Hunting, walking.
Abraham Lincoln	Billiards, cockfighting, marbles, walking, weight lifting, wrestling.
Andrew Johnson	None. He wasn't particularly interested in sports.
Ulysses S. Grant	Baseball, diving, horse racing, skating, swimming.

PRESIDENT	FAVORITE SPORT(S)
Rutherford Hayes	Croquet, hunting.
James Garfield	Billiards, horseback riding, walking.
Chester Arthur	Canoeing, fishing, hunting, swimming.
Grover Cleveland	Billiards, fishing, hunting.
Benjamin Harrison	Hunting, ice skating, fishing, baseball.
William McKinley	Fishing, golf, horseback riding, ice skating, swimming, walking.
Theodore Roosevelt	Boxing, exploring horseback riding, hunting, jujitsu, mountain climbing, polo, rowing, tennis, walking, wrestling.
William Howard Taft	Baseball (He was the first President to throw out the ball to open a major league baseball season), golf.
Woodrow Wilson	Baseball, football, golf, walking.
Warren G. Harding	Golf, table tennis, tennis.
Calvin Coolidge	Fishing, mechanical horse riding, trap shooting, walking.
Herbert Hoover	Baseball, fishing, football.
Franklin D. Roosevelt	Canoeing, fishing, football, golf, horseback riding, rowing, running, sailing, swimming.
Harry Truman	Fishing, walking.
Dwight D. Eisenhower	Baseball, boxing, fishing, football, golf, horseback riding, hunting.
John F. Kennedy	Baseball, fishing, football, golf, sailing, swimming, tennis, touch football.
Lyndon B. Johnson	Boating, golf, horseback riding, hunting, swimming, walking.
Richard Nixon	Bowling, golf.
Gerald Ford	Golf, running, sailing, swimming, skiing.
Jimmy Carter	Canoeing, fishing, running, softball.
Ronald Reagan	Horseback riding, swimming.

U.S. Presidents Depicted on Money

Coins

1 cent	Penny	Abraham Lincoln
5 cents	Nickel	Thomas Jefferson
10 cents	Dime	Franklin Delano Roosevelt
25 cents	Quarter	George Washington
50 cents	Half-Dollar	John F. Kennedy
$1.00	Dollar	Dwight D. Eisenhower

Paper Currency

$1	George Washington
$2	Thomas Jefferson
$5	Abraham Lincoln
$20	Andrew Jackson
$50	Ulysses S. Grant
$500	William McKinley
$1,000	Grover Cleveland
$5,000	James Madison
$100,000	Woodrow Wilson

U.S. Savings Bonds

$25	George Washington
$50	Franklin Delano Roosevelt
$75	Harry S. Truman
$100	Dwight D. Eisenhower
$200	John F. Kennedy
$500	Woodrow Wilson
$1,000	Theodore Roosevelt
$5,000	William McKinley
$10,000	Grover Cleveland

Sports

"The important thing in the Olympic Games is not to win, but to take part; the important thing in life is not the triumph but the struggle; the essential thing is not having conquered but to have fought well."
—BARON PIERRE DE COUBERTIN,
father of the modern Olympic Games

Olympic Sports

The Olympic Games are the ultimate competition for the amateur athlete. They are held every four years in various countries throughout the world.

Olympic Facts

Olympic Symbol: The five circles represent the following continents: Africa, the Americas (North and South), Asia, Australia, and Europe. They are interlocking to show friendship among the people of the world. The colors of the rings—blue, yellow, black, green, and red—were chosen because they are commonly found among the flags of all the countries of the world.

Olympic Motto: "Citius, Altius, Fortius" (Faster, Higher, Stronger).

Olympic Creed: "The most important thing in the Olympic games is not to win but to take part, just as the most important thing in life is not the triumph but the struggle. The essential thing is not to have conquered but to have fought well."

Olympic Hymn: "The Hymn Olympique" (composed in 1896 by Spyro Samaras of Greece).

Olympic Prizes:
  Ancient
     —First Prize—Laurel wreath
      Second Prize—Wild olive wreath
      Third Prize—Palm wreath
  Modern
     —First Prize—Gold medal
      Second Prize—Silver medal
      Third Prize—Bronze medal

Olympic Athletes: Each athlete represents a country; however he or she competes and wins as an individual. The only restrictive requirement for competitors is that they must be amateur (unpaid) athletes.

Countries Represented in the Olympics: Ancient Olympics—one country (Greece).

First Modern Olympics—Thirteen countries.

Present-Day Olympics—more than 120 countries.

The Official Olympic Sports

Summer Sports

Archery—Men, Women

Basketball—Men, Women

Boxing—Men

Canoeing—Men, Women

Cycling—Men, Women

Equestrian Games (horse riding)—Men, Women

Fencing—Men, Women

Field Hockey—Men, Women

Gymnastics—Men, Women

Judo—Men

Modern Pentathlon (cross-country running, fencing, riding, shooting, and swimming)—Men

Rowing—Men, Women

Shooting—Men, Women

Soccer—Men

Swimming and Diving—Men, Women

Track and Field—Men, Women

Team Handball—Men, Women

Volleyball—Men, Women

Water Polo—Men

Weightlifting—Men

Wrestling (freestyle and Greco-Roman)—Men

Yachting—Men, Women

Winter Sports

Biathlon (skiing and shooting)—Men
Bobsledding—Men
Figure Skating—Men, Women
Ice Dancing—Men, Women
Ice Hockey—Men
Luge (sledding)—Men, Women
Skiing (Nordic and Alpine)—
  Men, Women
Speed Skating—Men, Women

OLYMPIC SYMBOLS

Olympic sports pictograms © 1981, Los Angeles Olympic Organizing Committee

Olympic Games Timeline

B.C.

776   The first recorded Olympics were held in Olympia, Greece. There was only one sporting event. It was a race of 200 yards. These Olympics were held for 1,168 years—a total of 242 Olympiads.

A.D.

394   The ancient Olympic Games were banned by the Romans.

1896   The first modern Olympic Games were held in Athens, Greece. Baron Pierre de Coubertin, a Frenchman, founded the Games to foster sportsmanship among athletes and to create good will among people of all countries.

1900   Women were allowed to compete in the Games. Six women participated in lawn tennis.

1920   The Flight of Doves was officially introduced to the opening ceremony of the Olympics.

1924   The winter Games were held for the first time. They were contested at Chamonix, France.

1928   The Olympic torch was lit for the first time at the Amsterdam Games.

1936   These were the first televised games and included the first lighted torch relay—from Olympia, Greece, to Berlin, the site of the Games.

1969   Athletes who participated in women's events were required to take a femininity control exam, to be sure they were women.

1984   The summer Games became the most televised in history when ABC (The American Broadcasting Company) bought the rights to show 200 hours of sports over a 2-week period.

Memorable Olympic Athletes

Vasili Alexeyev, U.S.S.R.
This 345-lb. superweight set a
world record when he lifted
562 lbs. to become the world's
strongest man. He won gold
medals in the 1972 and 1976
summer Games.

Robert Beamon, U.S.A. His
29-foot, 2½-inch long jump at
the 1968 Olympics was hailed
as one of the greatest athletic
achievements. It was 21¾ inches
longer than the world record.

Joan Benoit, U.S.A. She won
the first Olympic women's marathon at the 1984 Los Angeles
Summer Games.

Abebe Bikila, Ethiopia. He
was the first to win the marathon twice, in 1960 and 1964.
He was also the first gold med-
alist from black Africa. In 1960,
he ran the entire 26.7-mile
marathon barefoot.

Francine Blankers, Holland.
This 30-year old mother was
known as "Marvelous Mama"
at the 1948 London Olympics
where she won four gold medals in track and field events.

Ethelda Bleibtrey, U.S.A.
She was the first woman to win
three Olympic gold medals in
any sport. She took the honors
in swimming at the 1920
Olympics in Antwerp.

Nadia Comaneci, Romania.
At the age of 14 she became the first gymnast to score a perfect 10. Altogether she won three gold medals, a silver, and a bronze at the Montreal Olympics in 1976. In Moscow, 1980 she won two more gold medals.

James B. Connolly, U.S.A.
He was the first person to win a gold medal in the modern Olympic Games. He won the gold in the triple jump in Athens, Greece in 1896.

Mildred "Babe" Didrikson, U.S.A. She was one of the first females to be an Olympic star. An all-around athlete, she won a gold medal in the javelin and the hurdles, and a silver medal in the high jump at the 1932 Olympics in Los Angeles.

Eddie Eagan, U.S.A. He is the only athlete to win gold medals in both the winter and summer Games. He won the first in boxing at the 1920 summer Games and a second in bobsledding at the 1932 winter Games.

Kornelia Ender, East Germany. She is one of the greatest female swimmers of all time. She won 4 gold medals at the 1976 Montreal Games.

Ray Ewry, U.S.A. Known as "the rubber man," this track and field star won an all-time record string of ten consecutive

Olympic championships from 1900–1908. His wins were in the standing high jump, standing long jump, and standing triple jump.

Dick Fosbury, U.S.A. He was the first Olympic high jumper to go over the pole head first, landing on his back. This style known as the "Fosbury Flop" earned him a gold medal in Mexico in 1968 and set a new trend in high jumping.

Shane Gould, Australia. This great swimmer won three gold medals, a silver, and bronze in the 1972 Olympics. She also broke world records in 3 swimming events in the same Olympics.

Eric Heiden, U.S.A. Considered the greatest men's speed skater in history, he won five gold medals in the 1980 Winter Olympics in Lake Placid. He was the only athlete to win five individual golds in the history of the Winter Olympics.

Sonja Henie, Norway. A world champion figure skater, she first competed at the age of 10 in 1924. She did not win that year but went on to win gold medals in the 1928, 1932, and 1936 Olympics.

Ivan Johansson, Sweden. The top Swedish wrestler, he won three gold medals in wrestling; two in 1932 and one in 1936.

Olga Korbut, U.S.S.R. This great Olympic gymnast won three gold medals at the age of 17 in 1972. At the following Olympics in 1976 she won another gold and two silver medals. She is famous for inspiring many youngsters to take up the sport of gymnastics.

Alvin Kraenzlein, U.S.A. He won four individual championships in 1900. He won the 60-meter spring, 110-meter high hurdles, 200-meter low hurdles, and the long jump.

Carl Lewis, U.S.A. He won four gold medals for track and field events at the 1984 Summer Games in Los Angeles. He excelled in the long jump, the 100 meter, 200 meter and the relay.

Bob Mathias, U.S.A. At the age of 17 he upset the field in the 1948 decathlon by winning the gold. He won again in 1952 and became the only athlete to win the decathlon twice.

Paavo Nurmi, Finland. The "Flying Finn" as he was called, set 22 world records, and won nine golds and three silvers in middle and long distance races. He participated in the 1924 and 1928 Winter Olympics.

Alfred Oerter, U.S.A. His record wins as a discus thrower have never been matched. From 1956 to 1968 he won 4 consecutive gold medals.

James "Jesse" Owens, U.S.A. The hero of the 1936 Berlin, Olympic Games, Owens won four gold medals in track and field. He is also remembered for Adolf Hitler's refusal to shake hands with him because he was black.

Tamara Press, U.S.S.R. She is one of the top field-event women in the world. Weighing in at 220 pounds, she won the shot put title in 1960 and 1964. In 1964 she also won the discus.

Peter Snell, New Zealand. He is remembered as the only athlete to win three Olympic gold medals in mid-distance races. He won two in 1960 and one in 1964.

Mark Spitz, U.S.A. He dominated the 1972 Olympics in swimming. He entered seven events and won seven gold medals in individual and team events. No athlete before him had ever won as many as seven golds in one Olympiad.

Oscar Swahn, Sweden. At age 72 he was the oldest person to win an Olympic medal. A legendary target shooter, he won three gold, one silver and two bronze medals in the 1908 and 1912 Olympics.

James "Jim" Thorpe, U.S.A. This native American was one of the greatest athletes of all time and the only one to win both the decathlon and pentathlon (1912). In 1913 his medals were taken away because it was learned that he played semi-professional baseball in 1909 (all Olympic participants must be amateurs). In 1982, twenty years after his death, Thorpe's medals were returned to his family. His wins were once again recorded in Olympic history.

Johnny Weissmuller, U.S.A. Considered the greatest swimmer of the first half of the 20th century, he won five gold medals in the 1924 and 1928 Olympics. Later, he became famous as "Tarzan" in the movies.

The Junior Olympics

This is the largest amateur sports program in the United States. It was designed to interest the nation's youth in Olympic sports. Competitions take place in towns and cities in every state. Youngsters 8 to 18 years old can compete only if they have never participated in competitive athletics before. There are competitions on local, state, regional, and national levels.

The Official Junior Olympic Sports

Baseball
Basketball
Bobsled-Luge
Boxing
Cross Country Running
Decathlon
Diving
Field Hockey
Gymnastics
Judo
Soccer

Swimming
Synchronized Swimming
Table Tennis
Tae kwon Do
Track and Field
Trampoline and Tumbling
Volleyball
Water Polo
Weight Lifting
Wrestling

Famous Athletes Who Were Former Junior Olympians

Basketball Players:
William Bradley, Jr.
Earvin "Magic" Johnson

Boxers:
Sugar Ray Leonard
Ken Norton

Decathlon Competitors:
Rafer Johnson
Bill Toomey

Gymnast:
Kurt Thomas

Runners:
Wilma Rudolph
Frank Shorter

Swimmers:
Donna DeVarona
Mark Spitz

For more information contact:
Junior Olympics
AAV House
3400 West 86th Street
Indianapolis, Indiana 46268

The Special Olympics

This is an international program of physical fitness, sports training, and athletic competition for mentally retarded people 8 years old and up. Participants are often active in year-round training programs. There are local and national games each year. The international games are held every four years at selected sites in the U.S.

The Special Olympics Sports

Basketball
Bowling
Diving
Floor Hockey
Frisbee-Disc
Gymnastics
Poly Hockey

Soccer
Softball
Swimming
Track and Field
Volleyball
Wheel Chair Events

The Special Olympics Winter Games

Alpine Skiing
Cross Country Skiing
Ice Skating
For more information contact:
Special Olympics
1701 K Street NW, Suite 203
Washington, D.C. 20006

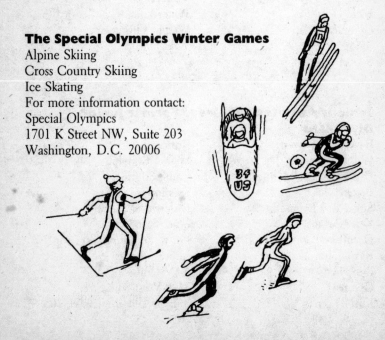

Weekly Reader Books